REVISED EDITION

How to Get Your Child a Private School Education in a Public School

c. 1

Martin Nemko, Ph.D.
with Barbara Nemko, Ph.D.

with a Special Note to Parents by Mary Ann Leveridge,
Past-president, National PTA

Ten Speed Press
Berkeley, California

HOW TO GET A "PRIVATE SCHOOL" EDUCATION IN A PUBLIC SCHOOL is
available directly from the publisher in individual and bulk quantities. For more
information regarding discount schedules and ordering, please write: Ten Speed Press,
Box 7123, Berkeley, California 94707.

1☺
TEN SPEED PRESS
P.O. Box 7123
Berkeley, California 94707

Book Design by Faith and Folly
Cover Design by Fifth Street Design Associates
Typeset by The Mac Studio

Library of Congress Cataloging-in-Publication-Data

Nemko, Marty, 1945—
     How to get a "private school" education in a public
school / by Marty Nemko & Barbara Nemko.
     p. cm.
     Includes bibliographical references and index.
     ISBN 0-89815-279-8: $12.95 ISBN 0-89815-277-1 (pbk.): $8.95
     1. Public schools—United States. 2. Parent-teacher
relationships—United States. 3. Home and school—United States.
4. Study, Method of. 5. School, Choice of—United States.
I. Nemko, Barbara, 1950—   . II. Title.
LA217.N45 1989
371'.01'0973—dc19   88-27736
                                              CIP

Printed in the United States of America
1 2 3 4 5 - 93 92 91 90 89

This book is dedicated to our parents,
and to all parents,
who care enough to use,
not just read this book.

A SPECIAL NOTE TO PARENTS

by Mary Ann Leveridge,
Past President,
National Parent Teacher Association

Dear Parents,

If every parent of every preschool and school-age child practiced the advice in this book, public schooling, as well as private schooling in this nation would be changed in a manner that no amount of legislative reform will ever achieve.

One might assume because of the high cost of private schools that they offer quality not possible in public schools. That is a myth! There are good and bad private as well as public schools. This book shows how parents can secure such excellence in education for their children in good public schools and escape spending thousands of dollars for private schooling.

This book is objective and practical, and springs from the wealth of experience of the authors. It also carries a message of hope.

Parents can get more for their child from the public schools. They can learn how to talk productively with the teachers and the school principal. Part I will assist parents in learning about the schoolwork required and the results achieved. Part II offers suggestions for dealing with homework, tests, peer group problems and stress. Part III will help parents to take action to ensure that their student has access to the best teachers and public schools in the area.

The public school institution, to a large extent, is the only business in town in which a purchase or attendance by the consumer is compulsory but in which the customer is never consulted or encouraged to have any choice or influence over the product or its delivery. But this book shows parents that they *can* have choices.

This book spells out goals and methods in plain English which is a refreshing and delightful experience after the arrogance of educationese. Millions of parents do care about the quality of schooling their children receive. At last here is a guide, a map and a "how to do it" book that makes sense.

Public education in this country has made a long and arduous journey since the early days of the nineteenth century when Thomas Jefferson asked the Virginia legislature to fund three years of school for the state's children.

The educational reform movement of the '80s may raise curriculum and grade standards but there is grave danger that it will be at the expense of the students least able to achieve any level of success. Individual differences will exist in children forever, and parents must insist that a full measure of opportunity be given to both gifted and academically slow students, as well as to the great mass of students labeled average.

Renewing the effectiveness of American schools will take place only after both the politicians and the educational community realize that schools belong to students and parents as well as to legislatures and school faculties. Contrary to the message of the wailing doomsayers and the media, there are thousands of excellent teachers and schools. Parents must scream with the same loud clamor as the media and must demand only the best teachers and schools for their children. That is educational reform.

Public schools touch the lives of more people than any other institution in our society. Each child deserves a school where he or she is somebody. Every school must be such a place. Parents and teachers working together to that end can preserve and transform the dream into reality.

Sincerely,
Mary Ann Leveridge

TABLE OF CONTENTS

CONTENTS

ACKNOWLEDGMENTS

It is often said that man* is selfish by nature. The falsity of this premise is clearly disproven by the remarkable generosity of the many people who helped make this book possible, most notably:

The educators who contributed so many innovative and practical ideas: Michael Scriven, Allan Gold, Don Arnstine, Phyllis Kaplan, Patrick Duffy, Emmy Werner, Bill Levinson, Steve Cederborg, Leo Gaspardone, Tu Jarvis, Ann Seasons, Marcie Radius, Dave Taylor, Delores Paz, Pauline Reno, Carole Scott, Roger Magyar, Aldo Fiammengo, and many other educators including the faculty of our daughter's school, Montera Junior High School in Oakland, California;

The many parents who tried out and helped refine the ideas in this book, with special thanks to Sandy and Mickey Silberman, Cal and Barbara Podrid, Judy Pence, Mark and Peggy Phillips and their wonderful children, Katharine, Annemarie, and Andrew;

The people who helped make the writing clear and to the point: S.J. Stewart, Margaret Miner, Bruce Bennett, Lisa Nage, April Hechter, and my dear friend, David Wilens;

The Hendsch family for their Apple IIe and emotional support;

Al Hackl, Val Avedon, Sandy Trupp, Dan Wallace, Robert Hickey, Luther Nichols, Brad Bunnin and Judy Hilsinger for their help in publishing and marketing;

Our dear neighbor, the amazing Ernest "Ray" Mattoon, who despite having no particular training in education, contributed enormously to this book, both in ideas, and editorially. He gave us over 100 pages of feedback on the book! He also fixes the plumbing in our house on a regular basis;

*We use 'he' as an indefinite pronoun in the traditional way but mean no bias. We urge readers to use common sense in removing mental gender barriers as they read.

ACKNOWLEDGMENTS

Our daughter, Amy, a good student and more importantly, a good kid, who has managed to tolerate graciously fifteen years of being the guinea pig for our ideas on education; and

Finally, central to any successes we may have are my parents, Boris and Seva Nemko. Both of them survived years in a Nazi concentration camp after which they immigrated to America, unable to speak a word of English. They have triumphed over all to make a happy and successful life for themselves and their family. They will always be a source of inspiration to me.

INTRODUCTION

P.S. 173
versus
The Bentley Academy

*We waved goodbye to our bright-eyed
kindergartener. Now we say "hello" to a
dulled second grader.*

A PUBLIC SCHOOL PARENT

Are you concerned that the public schools might dull your bright-eyed child? As educators, former public school teachers, and parents ourselves, we know it can happen. But, many children receive a first-rate education in the public schools. A *Science Digest* survey of the nation's 100 most promising young scientists revealed that 81 were educated in public schools. Two-thirds of students at Ivy League colleges come from public schools.

Some children get a good public school education by chance—they happen to attend particularly good schools and get more than their share of good teachers. But why take potluck? As insiders, we have learned how to *ensure* that our children receive an excellent education in the public schools. This book will show you how to do it within the public schools of your area.

If you've been resigned to spending thousands of dollars each year for private school, this book can give you a choice where you thought none existed. If private school isn't an option for you, this book can reassure you that your child needn't be short-changed just because he attends public school.

1

Many parents think this is impossible. They believe private schools enjoy at least three insurmountable advantages over public schools: more academically oriented students, more individual attention, and better teachers. In each case, the advantage may not be as real or insurmountable as it may seem. In comparing public schools favorably to them, we don't mean to denigrate private schools. We merely wish for parents to consider that a private school might not be thousands of dollars a year better than at least one nearby public school. (This implies that you're not limited to your regularly assigned public school. Later, we will show how you may indeed be able to get your child into other schools.)

The Pro Private School Arguments

"Private schools have more academically oriented students."

Let's examine these supposed advantages of private school. Here's how one private school parent expressed the "more academically oriented students" argument:

> If your child is academically oriented and the school is filled with students who aren't, your child may suffer. I realize that private schools attract some problem children, kids who didn't do well in public school and need special attention. But, in general, private schools have better students because the public schools have to accept everyone while private schools can handpick their students and ship any problem students back to public school.

Many parents use such reasoning to conclude that they should send their children to private school. However, these parents may be overlooking an important point: no child really attends a whole school. The students who count are those in his class. He receives all of his instruction with children in his class and primarily eats lunch, plays at recess, and makes friends with children in his class. If each year, your child's class has lots of reasonably academically oriented children, what goes on in the rest of the school will have little effect on him.

2

So the question is not, "Is the overall student quality equal at public and private schools?" but "In a public school, can one consistently get one's child into classes with academically oriented children?" The answer is usually yes, if you can get him into a school with ability-grouped classes (we'll show you how). Why are ability-grouped classes the key? If academically oriented students are grouped together, and your child is at least somewhat academically oriented, your child will have generally good classmates. (If your child is a poor student, you might consider a school that doesn't group classes by ability.)

We know of a child who attended a good public school through grade four. The school had four classes per grade level, and, each year, this child was placed in the highest level of the four, comprised of the top 25 percent. For the fifth grade, her parents transferred her to an elite private school. Unfortunately, its small size meant that there were only two fifth-grade classes. Although she was placed in the higher achieving one, it was still too low-level for her—the class consisted merely of the upper 50 percent of fifth graders, a wide range of students. Midyear, her parents transferred her back to the public school, where she found the students better and the work more challenging.

This is not to say that students in your child's class will necessarily be better in public school, only that public schools may merit your consideration if you're choosing private school in order to get better students. Indeed, our daughter's public school has many less-than-exemplary students, but the students in her classes are generally very good, the equal of those in a fine private school. She gets an additional bonus in attending a public school in that in physical education, music, and recess, she has an opportunity to learn, firsthand, how to deal effectively with a wide range of people, a skill more easily learned in childhood, and much needed in adult life.

This book shows how you can tell if your child's classes, school, or potential new school has the critical mass of academically oriented students, and if not, how to get your child better placed. It also demonstrates some tools you can teach your child for thriving not just surviving, among the typically more diverse students in public school.

3

"Students get more attention in private school."

A second reason parents use to justify the expense of private school is to get more teacher attention for their children. These parents believe that private schools' smaller classes and the parents' substantial financial commitment will encourage teachers to develop closer relationships with students and recognize and address their needs.

On average, a child in a private school may, indeed, get more attention than one in a public school. But this doesn't mean a parent *can't* get his child private school attention in a public school. In fact, many parents do. We'll show you how to do it and how we've done it for our own daughter, without undue time and effort.

"Private schools have better teachers."

The third major reason parents cite for sending their children to private school is to get better teachers. Indeed, the quality of private school teachers is increased because private schools can dismiss incompetent teachers without the complicated due-process procedures that have resulted in the firing for incompetence of only eighty-six public school teachers from 1939 to 1982 in the entire United States.

Also, private schools can choose from teachers that public schools don't have access to: teachers who don't hold a teaching credential, who don't want to deal with the higher percentage of problem children found in the public schools, or who want to avoid the administrative hassles public school teachers often face.

On the other hand, before paying thousands a year for private school, consider that private schools get many teacher applicants who are rejects from the public schools. Given a choice, many teachers prefer to teach in the public schools because of generally higher salary, benefits, and job security. The average public school teacher's salary is 18 percent higher than for private school teachers.

Another plus for public school teachers is that they all must have teaching credentials. Not only does this mean they have taken many teacher training courses, but is also a measure of their commitment to teaching. Someone can decide to teach in a private school on the spur of the moment. We know a botanist who was unable to find a job in his field, and at the last moment, applied for and got a job teaching biology in a prestigious private school, even though he had no training or experience as a teacher. We're not saying that public school teachers are better than private school teachers, only that they aren't unquestionably inferior either.

But the parent who is concerned about getting good teachers for his child shouldn't be so concerned about the *overall* differences between public and private school teachers. As Lee Cronbach, the eminent educator from Stanford University pointed out, trying to figure out whether teachers are better in private schools or public schools is like asking whether one gets better food at home or at a restaurant: it depends on who's doing the cooking.

The more relevant question is, "Can I get my child into public school classes with teachers as good as those in a fine private school?" If that is the question, public schools may have an advantage over private schools since public schools are generally larger and, therefore, offer a larger choice of teachers per grade level or per subject. So, it would be a real plus for public versus private school if parents could handpick their child's teachers, or at least avoid the poor ones.

Parents have long tried to do so, with varying success. Some think that to be allowed to choose, they must be active in the school so the principal feels obliged to grant their requests. This can work, but many parents don't have the time. Fortunately, there are many other ways. We'll show you what we've learned as public school insiders and parents, and from interviewing principals as well as successful and unsuccessful parents about how to tell who the right teachers for your child really are (hearsay is so often wrong) *and* how to get your child placed in their classes.

In sum, a private school education cannot be viewed as uniformly and unalterably superior to a public school education. We'll show you how to get, in a public school, the elements most sought after in a first-rate private school.

An Overview

How to Get Your Child a "Private School" Education in a Public School will tell you more than that. It is a comprehensive guide to any child's education. Part I, "How to Get Your Child 'Private School' Attention in Public School," shows you how to raise your child from anonymity to positive prominence in the teacher's mind. It then explains how you can encourage teachers to meet your child's individual needs to the extent associated with fine private schools. Part I answers questions that parents repeatedly ask, such as:

- When I get concerned about something the teacher is or isn't doing, I'm reluctant to contact her about it for fear of alienating her. What can I do?
- There are thirty-two children in my child's public school class. How can I interest the teacher in my child so his needs don't get lost among the other thirty-one?
- My child is having a problem in school. What is the best way to approach it?
- How can I have school conversations with my child that are more informative than, "What did you do in school today?" "Nothin'."?
- What does that B on my child's report card really mean?
- How do I interpret that string of numbers they call "standardized achievement test scores"? Are scores at the 75th percentile good enough?

No matter how much attention a child gets from his teacher, especially in public school, he needs tools for student self-sufficiency. Without having to turn your athlete into a scholar, or your average learner into a genius, Part II, "Helping Your Child Thrive, Not Just Survive in Public School," explains how to show your child these tools for school success. You needn't tackle them all. You can pick and choose as the need arises. If your child is having trouble getting his homework done, read or discuss that section with him. If he's having trouble getting off to school in the morning, read or discuss that section with him. Part II answers such questions as:

- How can I help my child become more interested in school books than in school clothes?

- School mornings are madness in our house. Are there ways to make them easier?

- My child has trouble paying attention in school. What can help?

- What can help my child become more organized?

- My child doesn't seem to know how to study for tests. Are there any tips?

- Some kids seem to be great test takers. What do they know that my child doesn't?

- Are there any secrets to making friends in school?

- My child is sometimes bothered by the school bully. Telling the teacher doesn't do any good. What should we do?

- How do I figure out if my child really needs help with homework?

- If he really needs my help with homework, how can I provide it quickly and without tears?

- My child gets by a long assignments. What can help?

Part III, "Choose Your Child's Public School and Teachers," is probably the most important part of this book, presenting the information most central to getting a "private school" education in a public school. This information comes from a variety of sources. We interviewed many principals and school district officials, as well as parents who were and weren't able to get their child into a public school or teacher's class of their choosing. We reviewed the latest research and also drew on our extensive personal experience, both as educators and as parents.

In Part III, we distill this information into the School Report Card and the Teacher Report Card, practical tools parents can use to decide if a teacher or school is right for their child.

Part III also shows parents how to get their child admitted to a public school other than the assigned one. Part III shows parents they are not stuck! It answers some of the most important questions parents ask about their children's education, for example:

- I'm afraid that my child won't get a good education in the large, sometimes rowdy classes of public schools. Do I really have an option other than private school? There's a good public school a few miles from our home, but it's not our assigned school. We tried to get him in, but were denied. Are there some other legal ways to get him admitted that we might not know about?

- Our state policy now allows parents to send their child to any public school in the state. But with all the restrictions, I still don't seem to have much choice. What can I do?

- We're moving to a new area. Can I choose my child's school simply on reputation?

- My child attended the local public elementary school, but I'm not sure I want him in the local public junior high school. Do I have an alternative other than an expensive private school?

- I want my child to get a good teacher next year, but I'm not sure who the right one for my child is. How can a non-educator find out without having to spend hours observing in the classroom?

- My child is doing poorly in school this year and hates his teacher. I'm wondering if I should get him transferred. How should I decide?

- My daughter is going into the fourth grade next year. I know that one of the fourth grade teachers is wonderful and the other is horrible. I want to ask the principal if he'll put my daughter in the good teacher's class, but I've asked before and he said, no. What should I do?

Although developing the ideas for this book has taken our forty-one years of experience as educators—insiders—and as parents, consolidated with information from other professionals and parents, the ideas themselves are relatively simple and straightforward. In essence, the information and techniques we present make *you* insiders, too.

The ideas are easy to put into practice, taking far less time and energy than dealing with an unhappy child who hates school or is having problems there. Like most parents, we are busy. Sometimes it seems as though spare time exists only in theory. So, in our recommendations, we have tried to make every moment count, to enable you to get an excellent education for your child with minimum time and effort.

The recommendations are time-effective largely because they don't ask you to remake your child or his teacher into someone else. They don't ask that you turn a school upside down. Instead, we accept your child and the schools for what they are and show you how to make the best of both.

A Personal Experience

How to Get a "Private School" Education in a Public School is not an academic exercise. We've field-tested these techniques with other parents as well as with our own daughter. When it came time to send her to school, we were living in a large urban area, and were a bit nervous about sending her to public school. We visited some nearby public schools and also some well-reputed (and expensive) private schools in the San Francisco Bay Area. As we expected, we saw some pretty bad public schools, but we also saw some that offered an education equal or superior to that offered at any of the private schools.

While the private schools generally had modern facilities, a large library and computers (both appeared largely unused), and swimming pool and tennis courts (heavily used) nestled into picturesque surroundings, what went on inside the classroom was less impressive. We saw plenty of kids slumped in their chairs and watching the clock as they plowed through such sedatives as "Wings of Learning" pages 37-44, long division problems, and looking up definitions to "igneous," "metamorphic," and "bituminous."

Some public schools were like this and worse: chaos in the classroom, with frazzled teachers begging in vain for students' attention, or explaining the same concept for the third time to the boredom of some and puzzlement of others. One fourth-grade class for gifted students was reading a second-grade-level book.

But at our public school of choice, most classes were filled with children who seemed absorbed, working hard yet content. One class, guided by an enthusiastic teacher, was debating the best plan to solve Africa's economic problems. Another class was figuring out the probability of drawing a black marble from a bag of multi-colored ones. When the teacher asked a question, an arsenal of arms shot up, straining toward the ceiling, with voices pleading, "Oooh, ooh, I know!" A third class was puzzling over how to design an experiment proving that water contained oxygen. The teacher had to pry them away when the recess bell rang. Although we certainly saw intelligent students in the private schools, we were surprised to find that, on average, the students seemed brighter and the level of instruction higher in the top level classes in our public school of choice. We knew we could put her in that school without feeling guilty (and save $5,000 a year).

That school was not our assigned school so we had to obtain an intradistrict transfer to get her admitted. (Chapter 10 shows many ways to get one.) Over the years, we used many of the other recommendations in this book: we chose some of our daughter's teachers, made the kinds of teacher contacts that would ensure that she was getting the most from each teacher, used some simple but not readily apparent ways to keep track of how she really was doing in school, and taught her some tools for thriving in public school. The result is that she has received what we think is an Ivy League prep education at urban public schools.

Beyond simply helping your child, reading this book will make you something of a connoisseur of good education, or at least a knowledgeable consumer. If you choose to be active in your child's school, you can use your connoisseurship to improve the education for all the children.

This isn't a book of miracles. It doesn't guarantee your child's success in school or that you'll be able to turn a mediocre school into a wonderful one. But we believe that its ideas can help get your child a fine "private school" education. In a public school. Free.

PART I

How to Get Your Child "Private School" Attention in Public School

It's a shame. No, Greg didn't drop out of high school or end up in jail. His school record card tells much of the story and his parents filled in the details.

Greg began elementary school with all the prerequisites for school success: he graduated Magna Cum Sandbox from a good Montessori preschool, he made child's play of the kindergarten readiness test, he liked kids and kids liked him.

In the first grade, though, something happened which would affect him into adulthood: he learned to read at an average rate. He was placed in the average reading group. He did fine, but that group only finished book seven while the fast group finished book nine. So next year, he was again placed in the average class and did fine. A child who somehow stood out may have been moved into the advanced class, but Greg was neither too loud nor too quiet, did his work but wasn't the type to fight his way into a higher group. So he stayed. And he did fine. All the way through high school. He now works at a local hardware store, doing fine. Greg turned out average.

Some parents would be satisfied with average, but Greg's parents had higher aspirations for him. Of course, many factors influenced Greg's life, but we can't help but think that his problems began back in the first grade.

Even if getting lost in the shuffle doesn't permanently affect your child, it certainly can cause him unnecessary difficulties. For example, Jason, a sixth grader, described this math lesson in his class:

> When Mrs. Daro started by saying that we were going to learn how to compute interest using our knowledge of percentage, I freaked! I had no knowledge of percentage. Then, as if I didn't have enough problems, Daryl, the kid next to me, started bothering me again: "Hey, did you see *The Texas Chainsaw Massacre* on HBO last night?" I told him to shut up, but he wouldn't stop until Mrs. Daro said, "You two back there, pay attention!" Not only does Daryl keep me from paying attention, he gets me in trouble, too!

Even though Jason, a pretty good student, would probably have survived anyway, he certainly could have used some attention from the teacher: he needed some help on percentage and needed his seat moved away from Daryl.

It's easier for children to get such attention in the small classes of expensive private schools. We'll explain three ways to help your child get this "private school" attention in a public school:

1. **Raise your child from anonymity to the teacher's favor.** Of course, your child's actions largely determine his status, but you can do some important things to help.

2. **Learn your child's needs.** There may be some skills your child should have but hasn't gotten out of school. These needs can go unnoticed in large public school classrooms, but you, who can focus on the needs of your child, can uncover them if you know what to look for.

3. **Get your child's needs met.** You can get the teacher to address these needs if you know *how* to ask.

CHAPTER ONE

From Anonymity to Under the Teacher's Wing

My sixth-grade teacher used to talk to me
after school sometimes. She made me realize
I could be somebody even though I was
'just' a girl

A PHYSICIAN

Your child's life can be changed by a teacher's special interest. A teacher's attention can give a child the confidence to turn on to learning, to conquer a long-standing roadblock, or to see a new career direction. At least, that child will gain from the extra help or enrichment. Many adults credit part of their success to the attention they received from a caring teacher.

While it may be easier to get this attention in the small classes of a private school, it is possible to get "private school" attention in a public school. The key to getting more teacher attention is to stand out from the rest of the students in the teacher's mind. But what makes some children stand out? Being unusually angelic or devilish helps, but what if your child is somewhere in between? Is he relegated to anonymity among the throng?

If you put yourself in the teacher's shoes, you will see how simple little things can raise a child from the anonymity of large public school classrooms to positive prominence in the teacher's mind.

What Can a Child Do?

First, let's look at things your child can do. Of course, being a good student is a certain teacher pleaser, but becoming a good student takes time. Fortunately, there are easier teacher pleasers:

- Many teachers view clothing as a sign of respect. My judgement of one student was probably altered because his typical school duds were an "Iron Maiden" T-shirt, tattered jeans, and a beret, only partially covering his greased hair.

- If your child has a choice, he should sit in a "power seat." Everyone knows it's easier to pay attention in the front seats, but there's more to it than that. Teachers tend to focus on the seats that are about 25 percent of the way back and slightly to one side of center. These "power seats" are the places to be. From there, the teacher is more likely to see your child's positive eye contact, his enthusiastic nods of agreement, his frequently raised hand, and that he's the first to pick up his pen and the last to put it down. Power seats are also great if your child needs help paying attention—it's hard to chat, doodle, or doze with the teacher's eyes beaming down on you every few seconds like searchlights.

- Teachers appreciate kids who sit up straight, wear a pleasant expression, and look right at the teacher when he's talking. They dislike a class full of bored faces slumped in chairs tilted back, with eyes everywhere but on the teacher.

- Your child should raise his hand as often as possible, especially when no one else is participating. It can't hurt to save a teacher whose lesson is drowning.

- Children sometimes forget that teachers are people, too. They have pet peeves and appreciate the child who makes an effort to avoid them.

- Your child should avoid being the last student to follow a direction. For example, when I said, "Let me have your attention," a number of kids may have continued talking for a few seconds, but it was the last one to stop that I noticed.

- Teachers enjoy kids who are good sports. Most classes have one or two chronic complainers: "It's boring," "It's too easy," "It's too hard." Kids need to accept that not all work will be just right. Of course, if the work is consistently too difficult or too easy, your child should inform the teacher, especially if there's a lower- or higher-level group in the class he could be moved to.

• If the teacher states an opinion and your child agrees with it, he might say so, but should think twice before disagreeing. Teachers, like to think of themselves as open-minded, but it's easy to get defensive amid a flurry of criticism. If the disagreement is important, your child should state it politely and, perhaps, privately.

• Your child should always keep something enjoyable yet acceptable to do in class for the inevitable times when he has nothing else to do.

• There are occasional yucky jobs that have to get done around a classroom—clean-ups, for instance. Teachers appreciate and are impressed with a child that volunteers to do them.

• Many kids take a teacher's efforts for granted. So, teachers appreciate the child who says, "Thank you for helping me."

• Your child might visit the teacher before or after class to ask a question, ask for help, even ask about his children. Most teachers like to spend one-on-one time with an eager, polite student. I know that I felt flattered when students wanted to spend time with me outside of class.

• Staying after school to help a teacher can offer particular benefits. The teacher may view it as a favor, and the child gets the rare opportunity to spend some good one-on-one time with the teacher. It's a good way to encourage a teacher to take a special interest in your child.

What Can You Do?

Now it's your turn. Here are ways that you can help raise your child from anonymity to positive prominence in the teacher's mind.

Parents with lots of spare time earn the attention for their child by becoming a classroom volunteer, PTA officer, or field trip chauffeur. This is impractical for many parents, but there are other approaches even the busiest parents can take.

As former classroom teachers, we know that parents who show support for the teacher somehow get more teacher effort for their child. Why? Teachers need lots of support because they're never sure how well they're doing. Lawyers know by counting up their wins and losses, salesmen by the amount of sales, and corporate employees by their promotions. In addition, in most professions, people earn words of appreciation from satisfied clients or bosses.

But teachers get little feedback. They don't know if their students turn out better than they would have with a different teacher. They never get a promotion, or a bonus and rarely hear from the principal or a parent—unless there's a problem.

So, if you let a teacher know you're on his side, he will appreciate and remember you, if only subconsciously. It might make a difference the next time he is deciding whom to call on, whom to help with seatwork, whom to give that good part in the play to, and whether to spend extra time working with your child.

A teacher usually doesn't make a conscious decision to give your child special attention, but it happens. Here's how one teacher put it:

> When a parent tells me how wonderful I am, I don't make a conscious choice to do more for that parent's child, I just somehow have a different feeling about him. I'm not even sure I do that much more, but somehow, if only from a glance or a few extra pats on the back, that kid feels special, not just because I appreciate his parent, but because he is special. I just might not have noticed if it weren't for his parent.

Here are some easy ways to show your support. Especially if you're pleased with your child's teacher, you can write him a kind note or two during the year. Imagine if you had to babysit, let alone teach, thirty children for six hours a day, five days a week, with rarely a thank you. Even waitresses get tips as a form of thank you. A note from a parent is like a well-deserved tip. Wouldn't you appreciate an occasional letter of support from a parent? Mightn't you remember that note when dealing with that parent's child?

When our daughter was in elementary school, we usually began each school year with a note such as this:

Dear Mr. Gade,

We're pleased that Amy will be in your class this year. We've heard terrific things about your critical thinking program. We both work full-time, so we can't help as much as we'd like to, but let us know if there's something you need donated or something we might occasionally do. Marty plays the piano rather well and, if you'd like, would be willing to do a little concert for the class.

Please feel free to call us for any reason.

Wishing you a happy and successful year,

Sincerely,
Barbara and Marty Nemko

Later in the year, if the teacher has done something we're particularly pleased with, we write a simple note, for example:

17

> Dear Mr. Gade,
>
> Amy has told us that you've been working with her on some science brain-teasers after school. We wanted to let you know how much we appreciate this and all your efforts with Amy
>
> Sincerely,
> Barbara and Marty Nemko
>
> c.c. principal

Teachers really appreciate our sending a copy of the note to the principal. Doing so also encourages the teacher to view us as connected with influence in the school: if we write a positive letter, might we also write a negative one if our child's needs aren't met?

Parents express their support in different ways. One parent of a child in my class made a one-time, few-hour commitment in which she called each parent in the class to develop a list of resources: parents who could come on field trips, those with time, skills, or items to contribute, those willing to teach the class about their job or hobby. These resources enriched the class throughout the year. I thought of this parent as helpful each time I used one of the resources even though the parent contributed nothing else all year. While, like most teachers, I tried to treat all students equally, my perception of this parent as helpful somehow translated into that child getting a little extra.

Another parent expresses her support of the teacher by giving her child's class a poster calendar at the beginning of each school year. This costs little money, time, or effort. Yet it quickly makes this parent's child stand out positively in the teacher's mind. It also helps the teacher fill a bulletin board, one of September's priorities. Further, the benefit is long lasting because a calendar is looked at all year, an ongoing reminder of the parent's interest and support.

Another parent gave the class a bag of flower bulbs. The class planted them in front of the school as a science project. The next spring, the long-forgotten bulbs surprised everyone with a lovely display that returned each year and reminded that teacher, and perhaps other teachers, of this parent's support.

Showing support is more than just giving things. For example, you can show your support by accepting a teacher's decision to discipline your child, even if you disagree with the decision. Let's say your child was late three days this week and, in anger, the teacher said he was going to lower your child's citizenship grade on his report card. The teacher probably overreacted, but if you make an issue of it, the teacher may hold a grudge, if only subconsciously. This can hurt your child more than a lowered report card grade.

Another key to getting attention for your child is showing that you care about your child's education. Unless you show that you care, on some level, the teacher may think, "If the parent doesn't care, why should I?" Here are a few simple ways to show you care:

- **Avoid unnecessary absences and lateness.** Try to schedule doctor's and other appointments after school or, if necessary, during school times usually devoted to nonacademic tasks. Remember that each time your child is absent or late, you make more work for the conscientious teacher—he has to explain individually or assign missed work, taking precious time from an already overcrowded school day. After a while, this could annoy even the most patient teacher.

- **Promptly complete and return all forms.** Teachers don't like having to waste time reminding students about, and collecting their late notes.

- **Help your child establish a daily routine that includes remembering school supplies** like homework, notebooks, pencils (with erasers), textbooks, etc. Teachers get understandably exasperated when the entire class has to wait while one child borrows the missing item.

So to summarize, you can help raise your child from anonymity to the teacher's favor in many ways:

- by teaching your child the "teacher pleasers" at the beginning of this chapter;

- by showing your support, perhaps by sending a kind note or two;

- by supporting the teacher on discipline matters, and;

- by getting your child to school regularly, on time, and with the needed paraphernalia.

These gestures will also motivate the teacher to tackle any unmet school needs you uncover. The next chapter shows you how to uncover them.

CHAPTER TWO

How is Your Child Really Doing in School?

Greg's parents thought he was doing well in school. Greg had a B average on his report card, most of the schoolwork he brought home looked good, he rarely complained about school, and his teachers said he was doing fine.

Greg's parents might have been right or they might have been wrong. While a B average in a top school would be quite respectable, grade inflation can give a C student a B average. The schoolwork he brought home could have been a representative sample but could also have been a handpicked selection of his finest performances. That Greg is not complaining about school means little—some kids who hate school rarely complain. Positive teacher conferences are no guarantee either. Some teachers will say a child is doing fine if he tried hard and isn't near the bottom of the class.

In short, Greg's parents didn't really know how well he was doing, and as you found out earlier, they needed to know, even though Greg was only in the first grade. Whether your child is in the first grade or the twelfth, in public school or private, it's worth keeping track of your child's progress.

Especially in large public school classes, teachers can have difficulty keeping track of each child's needs. You can help by uncovering your child's needs and tactfully sharing what you've learned with the teacher. Doing so is a key to getting your child private school attention in a public school. In this chapter, we show you how to uncover your child's needs, and in the next chapter, we offer tips for contacting the teacher.

Even if there's no problem, it feels good to know your child is doing well. It can reassure you that your child is getting a fair shake from a public school or that you're getting your money's worth from a private school.

You probably already use the right tools to find out how your child is doing: looking at his standardized test scores, report cards, and schoolwork, and talking with him and his teacher. But, too often, parents use these and still come away unclear about how well their child is doing. This chapter will show you how to better use these tools so you get a clear picture.

If you find that your child is having a problem, this chapter also explains a simple but powerful technique for solving school problems with your child that can eliminate unnecessary trips to the teacher, principal, or school psychologist.

Making Sense of Your Child's Achievement Test Scores

In most schools, instruction stops for a few days each year, not for a holiday, but so students can take a standardized achievement test. The results of this test give you a key piece of the puzzle: a comparison of your child's academic achievement with a norm group of children in his grade, a nice way to keep track of your child's progress and discover any problems. Unfortunately, the scores are usually reported via a complicated computer printout like the one below. (If you don't receive one within a few months of the test date, you can ask to see one at your child's school.)

Standardized Achievement Test Profile				
Jason Sage Happy Acres Sch. Grade 5 Test date: 4/20/86				
SUBTEST	R.S.	G.E.	NATL. %ILE	LOCAL %ILE
Reading Vocab.	41	7.4	88	74
Reading Comp.	41	7.7	94	78
Written Expr.	28	7.8	96	81
Written Mech.	45	7.2	86	71
Math Concepts	28	5.7	51	40
Math Comput.	26	5.6	48	36

Many parents, and even teachers, understandably have difficulty interpreting the results of these tests. This section shows you how to translate the above string of numbers into useful information.

Standardized achievement tests consist of a number of subtests, the results of which are reported in many ways, four ways in the printout above: raw score (R.S.), grade equivalent (G.E.), national percentile rank (%ile) and local percentile rank.

You only need be concerned with two of these, the national and local percentile ranks. These can give you a good idea of how your child did even if you don't have a degree in statistics. Percentile rank is the percentage of students at your child's grade level that got fewer items correct than your child did.

So, in the example above, Jason's national percentile rank on the math concepts subtest was 51 and his local percentile rank was 40. This means that 51 percent of a nationally representative sample of fourth graders did worse on the test than Jason while 40 percent of a sample of fourth graders in his school district did worse.

Here is a rule of thumb for interpreting your child's test scores:

Percentile Rank	Interpretation
1-20	well below average
20-40	somewhat below average
40-60	average
60-80	somewhat above average
80-99	well above average

But even this doesn't answer all the questions. For example, what does it mean to be "somewhat above average," or as one parent put it, *"My child's scores usually range between the 50th and 75th percentile. How good a college will admit him if he continues to score at these levels?"* This question is difficult to answer because college admission depends on much more than test scores, notably grades and extracurricular activities. But the following table shows, for various colleges, average student scores on the Scholastic Aptitude Test. (Note that colleges often have significantly lower requirements for minority applicants.)

Type of College	Average Student Scores
Ivy League, Stanford, Chicago ..	95+ %ile (1200+)
Berkeley, Notre Dame, Michigan .	70-95 %ile (1000-1200)
Moderately competitive colleges .	50-70 %ile (900-1000)
Low-competitive four-year private colleges	30-50 %ile (800-900)
Many two-year colleges	No or minimal test scores required

Then, there is the question all parents would like to ask: *"My child scores above the 90th percentile on almost all subtests, year after year. She's in the sixth grade and scores at the tenth or eleventh grade level. We can't put her in the eleventh grade. What do we do?"* First of all, grade-equivalent scores don't mean what most people think, especially those more than a year above or below grade level. If your sixth grader scores at the eleventh grade level, it doesn't mean that he can do the same work or is as smart as an average eleventh grader. It only means that he got as many items correct as the average eleventh grader might have *if* he had taken the test. In fact, no eleventh grader ever took the sixth-grade test. It is merely a statistical abstraction.

However, the question remains: what to do with the very high-achieving child? Indeed, some children who do very well on standardized achievement tests find on-grade-level work too easy. First, check to see if your child is, in fact, bored in school: talk with him or her and perhaps the teacher. Look at his or her schoolwork—are most errors careless or do they show lack of understanding? If you're convinced that your child is not challenged in school, you might try some home or school supplementation, or even a change of teacher, grade, or school.

Then there is the question of how much improvement in test scores justifies joy, how much decline warrants concern. One parent asked, *"My child did 5 percentiles worse than last year on reading comprehension. What does this mean?"* Probably nothing. If a child is given the same test two days in a row, his scores can easily vary 5 percentile ranks by chance alone. Look for changes of at least 15 percentile ranks.

Even a large change, under certain circumstances, can be meaningless. For example, in the fourth grade, as in most previous years, Sandy's vocabulary score was near the 50th percentile. In the fifth grade, she scored at the 20th. Her worried mother asked what she could do to improve Sandy's vocabulary that had declined so badly. A look at her answer sheet revealed that Sandy had skipped item 3 on the vocabulary subtest and proceeded to mark subsequent items in the wrong space on the answer sheet: the answer to item 4 in the space for item 3, the answer to item 5 in the space for item 4, etc. Rescoring her vocabulary subtest after moving her answers to the places she intended resulted in a score at the 53rd percentile, just where she always had been.

A spuriously low score can also be caused by other factors, such as illness, staying up late the night before, or misunderstanding the directions. In short, interpret your child's test scores cautiously, especially if they are markedly different from previous scores. Test scores are only one piece of the picture, and not the biggest one. A test score reflects only one brief sample of performance; it can't outweigh a child's classroom history and the tenor of previous test scores.

Here are some other common questions:

My child's scores usually range between the 30th and 50th percentiles. How do I know if he could be doing better?

Standardized tests measure achievement more than ability. So, look at other sources of information. Are there impediments to achieving his full potential: lack of effort, a poor school or teachers (judge these using the methods in Part III), social, emotional, or home problems? How bright does he appear in day-to-day life? How does he compare with the other children? What do his teachers think?

When do test scores really mean something?

Good scores are more significant than bad ones. Bad scores have many causes, but it's hard to get a good score by chance. So, if your child is in the low reading group and gets a high score on the reading test, it may really mean that he should be in a higher group.

Poor scores are significant only if they come in quantity—if your child scores low across the board on two test batteries in a row, it usually suggests a problem. Low scores might only reflect

25

test anxiety but they do warrant a close look at your child's schoolwork and report cards and a talk with your child and his teacher.

So what can Jason's mother learn from his standardized test profile? First, she should look for corroboration from previous achievement test scores. (It's a good idea to keep a file with all your child's test scores and his report cards.) If the pattern is consistent, she can conclude that, on this test, Jason performed well above the national average and somewhat above the local average on everything except math. In math, he is average when compared with national norms and somewhat below average when compared with local norms.

In general, it appears that Jason has excellent skills, so his mother should make sure he is not bored in school by talking with him and, perhaps, his teacher, and looking at his schoolwork. His scores give reason for optimism that his math weakness can be improved—his high scores on all the other subtests suggest above-average learning ability. Thus, some extra tutoring and effort might be expected to clear the problem up.

How Important Are Test Scores?

Many parents place importance on their children's standardized test scores. They are important. High scores open doors to challenging classes filled with motivated, well-behaved kids, and can mean admission to a desired college. But some parents stress the importance of tests so much that the child becomes unnerved in the test situation. This, of course, can cause lower scores—the exact opposite of what the parent intended. A parent's excessive expressions of concern about low test scores can also lower a child's self-esteem, making him feel that his low scores make him less of a person.

Achievement tests focus only on one aspect of a person—academics—an aspect that frequently assumes less importance in adulthood. An adult's success or happiness is often the result of qualities never tapped on achievement tests: perseverance, organization, knowing your limits, impulse control, and interpersonal skills. Help your child keep the importance of test scores in its proper perspective.

What You Can Learn From Your Child's Schoolwork

Most parents realize that looking at their child's schoolwork is a good way to keep track of how he's doing and to convey their interest in his education. But it's not always so easy. What if your child rarely brings home any work? What if he brings home lots of work except in math, which just happens to be his worst subject? What if he expects you to pore over sheaves of his work while listening to his detailed explanations after you've just returned from a long day at work? Besides, what exactly should you look for in those sheaves of papers? You've started to fill in the "How's Your Child Really Doing?" puzzle by looking at your child's achievement test scores. What pieces of the puzzle can you fill in by looking at your child's schoolwork?

Your child should be bringing home at least one piece of work per week in each major subject. If not, you can often increase the paper flow without the accusatory, "Why not?" by telling him something like, "I like seeing your schoolwork even when it's not so good, but I haven't been seeing much. Can you bring some more home?" That doesn't force your child to apologize or admit if he's been shielding you from bad papers. Don't argue if he says that his class does little written work, or that the teacher returns little of it. Just wait a few days. Often, papers start to trickle in.

If not, you might write a tactful little note to his teacher, for example:

Dear Ms. Paperhoarder

I like to look at Johnny's schoolwork to keep track of how he's doing. But he's been bringing home very little. Could you return some more of his work or if you already return a lot, let me know on the bottom of this note and I'll remind Johnny to bring work home. By the way, he has really been enjoying the stories you read to the class. Thank you.

Sincerely

Judy Miller

After a long day at work, we don't always look forward to spending lots of time looking at our daughter's work. We use an effective shortcut in which we focus on just two important questions:

Are most assignments complete? If not, why?

We scan our daughter's papers for subjects where much of the work seems incomplete or too short. If we find any, we ask why, using a tone of interest, not accusation. We'd be alerted to a possible problem if she frequently gave comments suggesting the work was too difficult; for example, "The teacher didn't give us enough time," "It was boring," "It was too hard," or "I hate that stuff."

Are there too many or too few errors?

Research suggests that learning is maximized when children get between 75 and 95 percent of the items correct on most schoolwork. Routinely getting more than 95 percent correct may indicate that the work is too easy. Frequently getting less than 75 percent correct suggests a need for help or easier work. Judging written work is more subjective. We simply look to see if the work seems adequate and note the teacher's comments.

Sometimes you can get an idea of the cause of a problem by asking your child if he didn't understand the concept, didn't memorize something, or was just careless. Or you could ask your child to explain how he got an answer to an incorrect item.

Because you're hunting for possible problems, looking at your child's schoolwork can easily become a negative experience. To avoid this, make a point of complimenting your child for any good work you see. In fact, try to start with a positive comment.

If we find uncorrected or minimally corrected work (for example, an essay that had no teacher reactions other than a few spelling corrections), we might scan it ourselves for errors. If over a period of weeks, lots of work was minimally corrected, we might write the teacher a polite note of concern about it:

Dear Ms. Uncorrector,

We periodically look at Tommy's work and have noticed that much of it appears to be uncorrected. We're concerned that without feedback, he'll continue to make the same mistakes again and again. Perhaps we're misunderstanding something and he's getting plenty of feedback. If our concern is unnecessary, please let us know. By the way, Tommy is so excited about his part in the play. Thank you,

Sincerely,
Mr. and Mrs. Samuels

Making the Most of Report Card Day

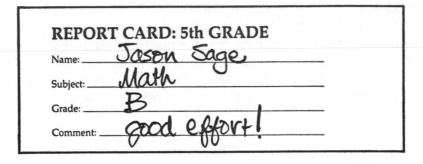

REPORT CARD: 4th GRADE

Name: *Jason Sage*

Subject: *Math*

Grade: *D*

Comment: *Needs Improvement*

REPORT CARD: 5th GRADE

Name: *Jason Sage*

Subject: *Math*

Grade: *B*

Comment: *good effort!*

Has Jason made great strides in math? That's the problem with report cards. You can't tell. Teachers' grading systems vary: some grade purely on achievement, others give credit for improvement or effort. Comments on report cards or in one subject, may signify a problem, especially if the same teacher gave both grades, but, in general, report cards aren't the best means of keeping tabs on your child's schoolwork.

But report cards are valuable for other reasons. Although we might prefer love of learning to fuel our children's schoolwork efforts, report cards are a prime motivator for many children. If that's true of your child, it's probably worth taking the time to examine report cards carefully with your child, meting out appropriate praise and concern. A report card does represent the culmination of months of your child's efforts.

Perhaps the most important value of a report card is that it evokes interest in even apathetic students. You can capitalize on this interest by using the report card as a springboard for uncovering any problems. For example:

Mom: Why do you think your math grade is so much higher than last year?[1]

Jason: I don't know.

Mom: Is it that you understand math much better this year?

Jason: Maybe it's because Mr. Weitz gives us extra credit for each bonus worksheet we do, no matter how many questions we get wrong. I've been doing real bad on the math tests so I do lots of extra-credit worksheets.

The Three-Question School Chat

The best way to keep track of your child's schoolwork may be to chat regularly with him about school. But for many parents the following is typical:

Parent: What did you do in school today?

Child: Nothin'.

Parent: Come on, you must have done something.

Child: Well, we had sloppy joes for lunch. They were gross!

Parent: What else did you do?

Child: We played dodgeball at P.E. You should have seen Tyrone's sneakers. They were soooh neat!

Not very illuminating. We listen to our share of these conversations, but when we want to know how our daughter is doing in school and try to address any problems, we use a "Three-Question Chat." We find it a helpful way to uncover, and often solve, school and other problems without taking up all the dinnertime conversation. The chat centers around three simple questions:

- What's the problem?

- What should we do about it?

- How will we know if it's getting better?

---

[1] Another example of the importance of keeping a file with all your child's school records.

We'll describe the Three-Question Chat in some detail because parents have found these details helpful. But don't treat them as lines in a script to be followed precisely. Successful problem-solving is often more affected by simple things like caring and good listening than by structural details.

What's the Problem?

Just listening carefully to your child will provide clues to problems: "Mom, I need help with my math," or "I hate Mrs. Malapede." In the absence of such openers, you can start a Three-Question Chat with an open-ended question like:

- If you could get rid of one subject, what would it be? (Children enjoy receiving in fantasy what is impossible in reality.)

- What do you like most and least about your teacher?

- What subject is the hardest (easiest)?

- Tell me what you did in school today, starting with the very first thing in the morning.

- Tell me the best thing and the worst thing that happened in school today.

If you already suspect a problem area, you might start with a question like:

- What did you do in math (reading, etc.) today? Did you understand it?

- How did you do on yesterday's _____ quiz?

- You were working hard on your _____ homework last night. Did you go over it in class?

- Are you still having problems with _____ ?

Don't forget about emotional or social problems:

- Did your teacher compliment or criticize you today?

- What did you do at recess?

- Whom do you like best (least) in your class? What do you like (dislike) about him?

Follow your child's response with questions to help you understand the problem well enough to figure out what to do about it. Don't jump to solutions too quickly—problems are often not what they first seem. Here's how Jason's mother homed in on his problem:

Mom: If you could get rid of one subject, what would it be?

Jason: Math.

Mom: Why?

Jason: Because I hate that kid Daryl that sits next to me.

At this point, Jason sees Daryl as the problem. Of course, his mother would be pleased if that were the problem—it wouldn't be Jason's fault and it would be easy to correct: just get his seat changed. But she knows she needs to ask more questions before accepting this as the root problem:

Mom: What does Daryl have to do with a math problem?

Jason: He bugs me in math.

Mom: Does he bug you in other subjects?

Jason: Yeah, but it doesn't bother me as much.

Mom: Why?

Jason: Because the other subjects are easier.

Mom: Math is hard, isn't it?

Jason: Yeah.

Now Jason and his mom have a general idea of the root problem. She continues to pin it down by asking questions and sharing relevant information:

Mom: Are you having a problem with one special thing in math or with most math?

Jason: I guess, with most math.

Mom: I think you're probably right. The math work I've seen hasn't been very good and your report card grades in math have been low this year and last. Is the problem better or worse than last year?

Jason: I'm not sure, but I think worse.

Mom: Do you have any idea why?

Jason: Well, because the work is harder.

She waits.

Jason: And because of Daryl bothering me.

She waits.

Jason: And because I sit way in the back of the room.

They've learned enough about the problem to move on to solutions.

What Should We Do About It?

Now, you can both share ideas on how the problem could be solved. Decide which ideas are likely to cause a lot of improvement for the amount of effort expended. Also, give preference to solutions that place major responsibility on your child rather than on the teacher or yourself, such as:

- finding a classmate to be a study buddy;
- working with a tutor;
- committing himself to trying harder;
- making and adhering to a study schedule;
- agreeing to study in a quieter environment;
- talking with the teacher if he needs help or believes she hates him;
- talking out a problem with an "enemy" child;
- reading more books for pleasure to improve a reading problem.

In Jason's case, a reasonable approach might have been for Jason to request to have his seat moved away from Daryl and toward the front of the room, and to promise to read, each night, the part of the math chapter that was discussed in class. Accepting responsibility for coping with one's own problems is a difficult lesson to learn. To help your child learn it, you'll have to give him assistance and lots of praise and hugs for his coping efforts, even when highly imperfect.

How Will We Know If It's Getting Better?

End a Three-Question Chat by agreeing on how and when you'll check to see if the problem has lessened. This can be as simple as, "Let's talk about math again in a few days." This ensures that the problem doesn't inadvertently get forgotten whether solved or not. It also helps your child feel that he's accountable for what happens. If, in a few days, the problem is still there, you can devise another approach.

Tips on Successful Three-Question Chats

- Try to have a Three-Question Chat fairly often, especially if your child is having difficulty in school, or appears anxious or unhappy. But make it brief. Two to five minutes is usually enough for one day. Much longer and both you and your child may begin to resent them.

- Choose a time when your child isn't otherwise distracted, perhaps dinnertime or bedtime. (What child refuses an opportunity to stay up a few minutes late?)

- Don't expect your child, particularly a teenager, to always be in the mood to talk. You won't always be in the mood either. But be concerned if your child's response to your school questions are usually uninterested or evasive.

- Keep having your Three-Question Chats even if you don't uncover problems. It's normal. Think of them like medical checkups. Even though the doctor always tells you everything is fine, you go, year after year, for that one time when he or she finds something which could get more serious without prompt treatment.

- Make it clear to yourself and your child that the purpose of the chat is problem solving . Since punishment and blaming don't solve problems, don't include them in your talks.

- Ideas should come from a true collaboration between you and your child. If you stray from fifty-fifty, let most of the input come from your child—you primarily ask questions. If you suggest something, ask your child what he thinks of it.

- Really listen to what your child says and look for the feeling message behind it.

- Take any report of a teacher's or child's misdeeds with a grain or two of salt. It has been said that grains of salt are necessary antidotes for a child's overstated or honestly misunderstood reviews of what happened.

- Silence is a valuable tool. Remaining silent after you've said something allows your child time to think about it. Remaining silent when your child finishes a statement lets him know you'd like to hear more about it.

- Balance your child's degree of concern with yours. If your child is overconcerned, be less so. If your child seems too cavalier, express more concern.

- It often takes time to arrive at a promising solution or even to understand the problem adequately. If you're not making progress, stop. A day or two can give you both time to think about it or to view it more objectively. Problems can even have a way of disappearing by themselves before your next school chat.

If You Can't Solve the Problem

Of course, Three-Question Chats can't solve all school problems. If the problem's serious, isn't going away by itself, you're out of promising solutions, or you simply need more information, decide whether you should contact your child's teacher or just live with the problem.

You may want to consider just living with the problem because you incur costs every time you contact the teacher about the problem:

- Each contact can move you down the scale from interested parent to pushy parent to "to-hell-with-her" parent.

- Pointing out your child's problems too frequently can encourage the teacher to think of your child as a problem child. This can become a self-fulfilling prophecy.

- A teacher will only give a child so many extras, even if the teacher is fond of him. Each time you ask the teacher to give your child an extra, you use one up. Don't waste an extra on something unimportant.

- Each contact tends to lower your child's self-esteem—it means he has problems he can't cope with himself.

- Each contact requires time and effort.

Is your child's problem worth incurring these costs? Yes, if it's serious enough to affect significantly his achievement or emotional well-being in a subsequent grade or in adulthood *and* is something the teacher can be expected to do something about. Remember that rarely can a teacher or even a parent turn a slow child into a scholar, an active child into a passive one, or a poorly adjusted child into a well-adjusted one. A good teacher can refine but rarely remold.

The following are examples of the kinds of problems that are usually worth contacting the teacher about:

- a standardized achievement test score below the 50th percentile, especially if your child did better on other subtests or if it's a new problem;

- failure to understand concepts that are key building blocks for later work; e.g., in math, the meaning of the ones and tens place;

- a marked decline in attitude, grades, or peer relations;

- ongoing reluctance to talk with you about school;

- frequent physical ailments on school mornings;

- chronic complaints about the teacher or schoolwork.

Unless it occurs repeatedly, even assuming you got the story accurately, think three times before contacting the teacher about something a teacher said or did; for example, accusing or punishing your child unfairly, giving an unfair grade, using harsh language, discussing a topic or espousing a view you think is inappropriate. These things are unlikely to cause your child permanent damage, but contacting the teacher about them might. At most, you'll get a grudging apology. Is an "I'm sorry for swearing in class" worth possibly turning the teacher off to your child? You often can mitigate any negative effects of a teacher's action, just by discussing it with your child. Of course, contact the teacher or, possibly, the principal if you suspect a more serious error, for example, continually severe punishment.

One more thing you may want to consider before contacting the teacher about a problem is whether the problem is yours or your child's? Our aspirations for our children often reflect our own strengths or wishes for ourselves. But our children are not clones of ourselves—your child may never be the scholar or athlete you are or wished you were. Erich Fromm, the social psychologist, said, "Few parents have the courage and independence to care more for their children's happiness than for their success."

CHAPTER THREE

Effective Teacher Contact

*Just walking into school makes me feel like
I'm twelve years old and in the sixth grade again.*

A PARENT

Wouldn't it be nice if your last teacher conference was this successful?

Teacher: Hello, Mrs. Smith. I'm glad you could come.

Parent: Thank you. How's Kevin doing?

Teacher: Quite well. He's doing fine in the top reading and math groups. If he has one area for growth, it's in spelling, but it's not serious. Frankly, if you hadn't come in, I might not even have mentioned it.

Parent: I've also noticed some poor spelling. Is there anything we can do to help?

Teacher: Well, in looking at his last few spelling tests it appears that he does fine with phonetic words but runs into trouble with the irregular ones. I think I could show him a few tricks that could help, but I probably won't have enough time during the school day. Could he possibly stay after school for about twenty minutes once or twice this week?

Parent: Of course. It's very kind of you to offer. Is there anything I can do to help?

Teacher: Actually, yes. I have this spelling workbook that I can't use in class because I only have a few copies. But it's very good and right on Kevin's level. Perhaps he could work on it at home when he has some spare time. Have him write the answers on a separate piece of paper so I can use the book again. If possible, correct it.

Parent: I'd be happy to. Thank you so much.

Teacher: You're welcome. Thank you for coming. It's been a pleasure meeting you. I'll expect Kevin after school one day this week and I'll do whatever else I can to help.

Parents often approach conferences with hopes of such a conference only to leave with an oversimplistic "Junior's doing fine" or a "Junior has a problem" without a promising prescription for cure. This chapter will show you how to get more from your teacher contacts, a key to getting "private school" attention in a public school.

Should you call, write a note, or have a face-to-face conference? Reaching out to touch someone either by phone or in person is well regarded these days. So, you may find it surprising that, at least if you're trying to solve a specific problem, you're probably best off trying a note first, even if writing isn't your forte. We know of too many conferences which accomplished nothing, or worse, annoyed the teacher so he took away, albeit unconsciously, any favored status the child may have attained.

A note can be successful because there's time: time to think before expressing or responding to an idea, time to diffuse a defensive reaction. How many times have we said something we wished we could take back? Also there's the time saved—face-to-face conferences take time, perhaps time taken from work.

The Three-Question Note

Your note can be structured much like a Three-Question Chat: "What's the problem?" "What should we do about it?" "How will I get your report?" Here's a note Mrs. Sage wrote to Jason's teacher about his math problem. Note how careful she is not to blame the teacher:

Dear Mrs. Daro,

A statement of her perception of the problem and request for the teacher's.

I'm a little concerned about Jason's math work, but I don't have the other children to compare him with. Is there reason for concern?

Implies the problem is not low general ability.

Jason's math scores are much lower than on other subtests. He said he doesn't understand some of the classwork and that Daryl, the boy next to him, bothers him mainly in math. He also says that he can't see the blackboard from his seat but he's too shy to tell you. What have you noticed?

Confines her comments to concrete observations, leaving the inferences to the teacher.

Concludes the "What is the problem?" phase.

We've tried going over problems he's gotten wrong and helping him with his homework but it hasn't helped much. What do you think might work?

The "What should we do about it?" phase.

Unless I hear from you first, I hope it's all right if I call you on Monday at 3:00. Thank you for taking the time to deal with this.

The "How will I get your report?" phase.

Sincerely,

Pat Sage

Often, your note will do the trick. Your thoughts may stimulate the teacher to try something or to suggest something you or your child can do. If so, call or write again in a week or two to see how things are progressing. But sometimes, the teacher may surprise you by viewing the problem differently, or even by suggesting a solution that you think is doomed to failure.

Your dismay might be justified, but take a few days to think about it. Remember that the teacher is a professional educator who sees your child more objectively than you, and knows what he can and will do within the realities of his classroom. If, after a cooling off period, you're still convinced that the teacher's response was inadequate, it may be time for another note or a conference.

Why Most Parent-Teacher Conferences Fail

Potentially, a parent-teacher conference can do wonders for your child. It can unearth and cure a school problem—or even a home problem—and can pique a teacher's interest in your child.

How can your conference achieve this potential? Most importantly, by minimizing anxiety and defensiveness so you and the teacher can be rational problem solvers.

Is there really that much emotion in parent-teacher conferences? Yes, and it's understandable. Your child reflects how good a parent you've been. If your child has a problem, especially a behavior problem, it's easy to feel that you're also being indicted. Also your aspirations for your child can make it difficult to accept that he has a serious problem—it's easier to blame your child's classmates or teacher. Most parents know they shouldn't become defensive, but the pressures of an on-the-spot conference can be testing.

A teacher's defensiveness is equally understandable. How would you feel if you were a teacher? Just babysitting thirty kids for six hours a day, five days a week would be a Herculean task. Imagine also trying to figure out, address all their learning, emotional, and social needs, too! Would you do a teacher's job, even if you did have the summers off?

Then after a long day of this, a parent comes in to talk with you about her Junior's problem. You know this can bring your teaching into question, if only by implication. You also know that as the "expert," you may be expected, yet be unable to solve the problem. Finally, you know that the parent will probably want you to change something about your teaching, a change which usually means more work for you. If you were the teacher, wouldn't you approach parent conferences with a bit of trepidation?

The result of all this emotion is that cooperation sometimes exists only on the surface of a conference. Mrs. Johnson may say, "Let's work together to solve this," but just below the surface can lie very different, often unconscious, feelings that can govern the proceedings. Especially if Mrs. Johnson feels threatened or that she is being asked to change, her subconscious may say, "She better not blame me or I'll have to blame her," or "I won't suggest anything that I would have to do. I've done enough already."

These feelings can undermine a conference, but your awareness of them is the first step toward controlling them and making your conference a success.

How to Have a Successful Conference

A major purpose of your conference is to share information about your child. To this end, some parents like to jot down information and bring it to the conference for reference, for example:

- a brief statement of the problem as you see it (be sure you state it as the child's problem, not the teacher's);
- a list of information related to the problem;[1]
- any solutions you've tried;
- any promising solutions you think are fair to ask the teacher to try.

Your conference will also be more successful if you approach the teacher in the proper spirit—as you would in asking a favor of a valued physician. Is this an unfair analogy? First, the teacher really is doing you a favor. He's not legally required to meet your child's individual needs. He may not even be required to meet with you.

The second part of the analogy, comparing the teacher with a valued physician, seems equally justifiable. Your child's teacher is in a good position to make recommendations about your child: he has years of training and experience in teaching children, and he sees your child every day in school where he can, with relative objectivity, compare your child with many others. You may have even selected this teacher for your child. Aren't his ideas worthy of the same respect you would accord a valued physician?

So, as in approaching a physician for advice, try to pick his brain; ask and listen much, say little. Try not to criticize, give advice, or express judgements of the teacher, positive or negative. The teacher doesn't want to feel you're standing in judgement of him.

---

[1] You may also want to bring relevant samples of your child's work or copies of his standardized achievement test scores.

Be prepared to hear some negative things about yourself or your child. You're emotionally involved, so it will be hard to tell if a criticism is legitimate or a manifestation of a teacher's defensiveness. Either way, defending your child probably won't help and can cause the conference to deteriorate into an argument. If you'll accept responsibility for part of the problem, you'll open the door for the teacher to consider change also. You can always reject the teacher's viewpoint later, but don't debate it during the conference. Take a few days to mull it over. The teacher may be correct.

A final key to preparing for a successful conference is to have realistic expectations for it. Don't expect revolutionary changes, either in the teacher or your child. Even principals find it hard to change a teacher. And unfortunately, few interventions, home or school, remake a child.

You can usually save much grief by basically accepting your child for who he is. We like to draw an analogy between a child and a black-and-white television set with a hard-to-turn channel selector. It's fairly easy to adjust the fine tuning, more difficult but still possible to change the channel, but impossible to change the television into a color set. You probably shouldn't approach a conference with the teacher expecting to turn your black-and-white television into a color set. Fine tuning may be the most you can expect, worthwhile in itself.

In sum, you'll be prepared for a good conference if you:

- have clear the information you want to share with the teacher;

- approach the teacher with the respect you'd give when asking a favor from a valued physician;

- don't defend your child or yourself when criticized, since that can quickly transform a conference into an argument;

- remember that your goal is to obtain information, information which can probably only fine tune, not remake.

Should Your Child Participate in the Conference?

In most cases, your child should participate in at least part of the conference. Sue Miller[2] explains via this analogy:

> Pretend you have a problem at work about taking an overly long lunch. Your boss calls your spouse in to discuss the situation. They decide you must eat at your desk for a week in order to repattern yourself. Your spouse returns from the meeting. You, who have been waiting anxiously, leap to open the door. 'What did the boss say?' Who needs the middleman? Not you, not your child.

Kindergarten and high-schoolers alike can benefit from participating. The child can better understand the problem, contribute information, and inhibit the parent or teacher from painting an overflattering self-portrait. He can profit simply from observing his parent and teacher solving a problem. Also, the teacher and parent can see the child in full dimension—the teacher can see how the child interacts with the parent, the parent can see how the child interacts with the teacher.

But your child needs a bit of preparation: he needs to understand that the problem is his, not the teacher's, that he can't criticize either the teacher or the parent, that he can give his view of the problem and propose a solution, but as a rule, should listen much and say little.

Making the Appointment

Write a note to the teacher requesting an appointment, offering a choice of days and times, and letting him know the topic you want to discuss. This enables him to prepare for the conference—consult records, keep a closer eye on your child, think about solutions.

The Conference: Preliminaries

Your first order of business is to try to minimize the "scared turtle effect." Unless the teacher feels safe and free from attack, he retreats into his shell to defend himself and that's a poor place from which to solve a problem.

[2] Miller, Mary Susan. *Bringing Learning Home*. N.Y.: Stein & Day, 1980.

You can help the teacher emerge from his shell as soon as you meet him. Dress neatly but not intimidatingly—leave home your attaché case and dress-for-success suit. Never come in angry; postpone the conference if necessary. Remember, you're approaching the teacher as you would in asking a favor of a valued physician.

Here's how Pat Sage's conference with Jason and his teacher went. Use it as a guide, not a script.

Teacher: Hello, Mrs. Sage, Nice to see you.

Pat: Thank you. Nice seeing you, too. Your classroom really looks lovely. I really like that art project on the bulletin board.

Starting her conference with a bit of chitchat can help the teacher understand that she's friend not foe.

To tell you the truth, I've been a little nervous about this conference. I wonder if I could have done more to avoid the problem Jason seems to be having.

It's difficult, but she can counteract the teacher's or her own scared turtle effect if she shares any conference-related feelings.

I'm hoping we can pinpoint the problem and then figure out what we might do about it. Does that sound okay to you?

Share your goals for the conference, using the same structure as a Three-Question Chat or note.

As I wrote in my note, I'm wondering if Jason has a math problem worth addressing? What do you think?

Start the "what's the problem?" phase.

Mrs. Daro: Actually, I think Jason is doing fairly well.

Teachers occasionally minimize the importance of a problem. If you're pretty sure there's a real problem, don't accept the teacher's reassurances. Instead, remind her of your evidence.

Pat: But his test scores in math are much lower than on other subtests. And look at some of his homework.

(Pat, Mrs. Daro, and Jason discuss the problem until they've defined it well enough to move to solutions.)

46

Teachers can lapse into educationese. Don't be embarrassed to ask the teacher to explain a term you don't understand. He usually will be glad to share his expertise.

Mrs. Daro: So it seems the main problem is that he doesn't understand place value.

Pat: Excuse me, but I'm not sure what place value means.

Mrs. Daro: Oh. I'm sorry. It's what the hundredths, tenths, ones, tens, and hundreds place mean.

Pat: Is there anything that can be done to help him with place value?

Try to get the teacher or child to come up with ideas knowing they're more likely to implement their own suggestions.

Jason: I can do the problems better using the unifix cubes I had in my last year's class. Maybe I could borrow them and use them until I understand place value better.

Mrs. Daro: That's a good idea. I'll ask your last year's teacher if I can borrow some. I also have some worksheets that focus on place value, which you can do for extra credit.

You may hope that the teacher might offer to give your child a little help before or after school but don't want to directly ask for fear of asking for too much.

Jason: Okay.

Pat: Sounds good. Do you think getting him a tutor for a while makes any sense?

Mrs. Daro: It couldn't hurt.

The "How will we know if it's getting better?" phase. You offer to call since a teacher is more likely to forget with a full class to worry about.

Pat: Is it all right if I call you in a week or two to see how he's doing?

Mrs. Daro: Certainly. The best time to get me is usually around 3:30.

Pat: Thank you so much for your time and effort.

After the Conference

It's a good idea to write the teacher a brief note of thanks. In addition to showing courtesy, it can remind him to do his part, and can diffuse any negative feelings the conference may have generated.

Sometimes parents leave even successful conferences disappointed. One reason is that they came in hoping the teacher could completely eradicate the problem with some in-school hocus-pocus. Unfortunately, teachers aren't magicians. Making a child a successful learner is often hard work, and the teacher can't do it all. You, and especially your child, have the main job. Try to get your child to do his part without nagging since he needs to know he's doing it for himself, not for you. Usually, your child will respond, though it may first take some more failures. Remember, too, that your child learns a worthwhile if painful lesson in personal accountability if he has to suffer the consequences of not doing his part.

If the Problem Persists

If your efforts have been unsuccessful, you may want to see the counselor, school psychologist, principal, or special educator. Ask your child's teacher to refer you to the person he thinks could be most helpful.

What if You Think the Problem is the Teacher?

Especially if all else has failed, you may think the teacher is at the root of the problem. You can check by making a classroom observation. The Teacher Report Card presented in Part III can enable you to learn more about a teacher from a twenty-minute classroom visit than from hours of unfocused observation.

Consider having your child transferred from the class if you're convinced the teacher is hurting your child and that another teacher would be much better. But be sure that the new teacher is worth a transfer's costs:

- Transferring can make a child feel that he can't cope with his problems.

- A transfer requires the child to adapt to a new teacher, new routines, and new students.

- If the problem doesn't improve after this rather drastic move, the child's self-esteem can suffer.

If possible, try to make coping with a poor teacher a learning experience. Since your child will encounter difficult people in his life, learning to deal with a poor teacher may be of value in the long run.

You can help your child make the best of a poor teacher by asking him to think of the teacher as a human being with human failings. Loving the teacher may be impossible, but tolerance isn't. As Sue Miller advises, your child can profit if he can develop the courage to show leadership in the class instead of joining the group of faultfinders.[3] By setting a good example, he can help establish a more receptive classroom atmosphere and make it easier for the teacher to relax and be his best self.

Even if you've decided to have your child stick it out, it may be worth seeing the principal about a poor teacher. The principal may feel he or she owes you one next year and make a point of placing your child in a good teacher's class.

How Much Time Does This All Take?

Amid all the explanations, it's easy to feel that getting your child "private school" attention in a public school is complicated and time consuming. It may be reassuring to summarize the plan:

- **Raise your child from anonymity to the teacher's favor** by showing your child some "teacher pleasers," showing your support of the teacher—perhaps by writing a complimentary note or two to the teacher, supporting the teacher's decisions to discipline your child, getting your child to school regularly, on time, and with the needed paraphernalia.

- **Keep track of your child's progress** by knowing what to look for in standardized achievement test scores, schoolwork, and report cards and knowing what to ask your child about school. You needn't do these things very often, only as needed to keep track of problems and occasionally as a checkup.

- **Get your child's needs met** by problem solving with your child, teacher, or other educational specialist.

[3] Ibid.

No matter how much attention your child gets from his teacher, especially in public school, he needs tools for student self-sufficiency. Without having to turn your jock into a scholar or your average learner into a genius, the following chapters show you how to teach your child these keys to school success.

PART II

Helping Your Child Thrive, Not Just Survive, in Public School

No matter how much attention he gets from the teacher, your child can use your help—not so much to help him learn, as to show him *how* to learn. We'll show you how to help your child become a self-sufficient student.

Especially if you have a touchy, nonacademic child who cares more about school clothes than school books, you may have some doubts: Can my help really make that much difference? Will making him a student take a lot of time and energy? Will he fight me every step of the way?

It's simpler than you may think, certainly less time consuming and draining than what many parents already do: spending night after night exhorting, cajoling, bribing, even doing their child's homework.

Importantly, you don't have to give your child the complete course on becoming the perfect student. Imagine you're taking your first tennis lesson. The instructor watches you hit a few balls and then, shaking his head, warns, "You'll have to change everything: your grip, position, backswing, swing, follow-through, and footwork. And that's just on your forehand." Unless you're unusually committed to mastering tennis, your racket may go back on the shelf before long.

Your child is probably no different. If you bombard him with the complete course on becoming the perfect student, he may soon drop the course, perhaps in favor of "How to Party in Public School." Fortunately, few children of parents concerned enough to read a book like this require the complete course.

These chapters contain a smorgasbord of ideas, any of which you can easily serve your child to make him a better student. Every so often, browse through the buffet and pick out an item to serve. You're never serving a whole banquet so your child is unlikely to say he's had too much to eat. Here's a menu of skills for thriving, not just surviving, in public school:

- How to help your child care more about school books than school clothes. (All of Chapter 4 is devoted to this. Chapters 5 through 7 cover the rest of the skills.)

- How to get your child off to school without morning madness.

- How to help your child be a recess success even if he's shy and not an athlete.

- How to help your child improve his classroom concentration.

- When paying attention is most and least important.

- How your child can take good notes without having to be a stenographer.

- How to help your child be a star classroom participant.

- What teachers really look for in written work.

- How to help even a sloppy child be organized enough for school success.

- Secrets of the successful test taker.

- How your child can deal with bullies and other hazardous organisms.

- How your child can minimize the damage when he's blown it.

- How your child should deal with "lost" pencils, papers, and books.

- How your child can finish all his homework and still have time for fun.

- How to know if your child really needs your help with homework and how to provide it, quickly and without tears.

- How he should study for a test.

- How he can write A papers with minimum pain.

Much of this information could be written in a book for students. But few children seek out such books. The information has a better chance of actually reaching students if you, the concerned parent, are the disseminator. It will be time well spent.

You may wonder whether you'll be able to convince your child to try even one of these ideas. It's difficult to convince some kids, but your best shot may be to appeal to his self-interest—that if he takes a little time to learn and try out these skills, he will actually save time, get teachers and parents off his back, and improve his grades. To help you with your sales pitch, we'll frequently point out, from the child's perspective, how using the skill is in his best interest.

Haven't We Done Enough Already?

Even though you know you can pick and choose from the above list, it may still seem overwhelming, especially if you're as busy as most of today's parents—it's one more thing you have to be responsible for. As parents ourselves, we know how difficult it is to be a good parent. It seems as though no matter how careful you are, you're always second-guessing yourself: "Was I too strict?" "Did I say the right thing?" "Will it permanently affect my child?" To make matters worse, how-to-parent books abound that make you feel guilty if you don't always follow their instructions. No one ever tells you you're a good parent, except, perhaps, if Junior has just gotten into Harvard.

But you probably are a good parent. After all, most parents concerned enough to read a book like this have already done much to prepare their children for school success long before they entered school.

Through visits to the pediatrician, you learned that your child's vision and hearing were normal. If there was a problem, you took care of it. You talked and talked with your child, knowing the importance of verbal interaction. You encouraged him to watch educational television and sent him to a good preschool. You gave your child self-help skills: he learned his full name, address, phone number, and parents' names. He could dress himself and use the telephone (though with direct-dial long distance, this may have been a mixed blessing). Finally, you made sure he generally appeared well turned out, knowing that teachers and students value an attractive appearance.

You bestowed all this on your child before he ever entered kindergarten. You've already done a lot. Nonetheless, some children who receive such excellent preparation don't do as well in school as they could if they had had some of the skills for thriving listed above. Scott, a bright boy who comes from a good home, is a somewhat extreme case, but spending a school day with him illustrates the point:

Scott was dozing while Mr. Richards was explaining pulleys, and he quickly paid a price when Mr. Richards asked each student to make a pulley out of some raw materials. Scott should have immediately asked for help but was embarrassed, so he just fumbled around with the pieces. After a while, the teacher noticed his plight. It was already late in the period, so Mr. Richards simply suggested that he ask for help earlier next time, and made a negative mental note about Scott.

For homework, they had to explain how someone unable to lift a hundred pounds could do so with a pulley. Also, there would be a test on simple machines the next day. Scott nearly choked but for the recess bell, the sound of relief.

But for Scott, recess brought its own pressures. He saw kids choosing sides for softball and would have liked to play but was shaky on the rules. So, rather than being exiled to right field and appearing foolish because he didn't know some rule, he spent his ten minutes roaming around, occasionally saying "hi" to kids he knew—he was one of those kids who often got stuck right after "Hello." His most extended interaction was when the school tough-guy decided to make Scott the momentary target of his amusement. Although Scott had been grateful to hear the recess bell, he didn't mind hearing the bell ending recess.

Before the day was over, the class received two more homework assignments, easy for most who paid attention, difficult for distractible Scott. At home, Scott was faced with play versus homework. He chose play, vowing to work extra hard after dinner, reasoning that he'd work better when rested.

Unfortunately, exhausted was more like it. Six hours of school followed by two hours of play and a heavy dinner made his homework loom enormous. But by 10:00, the daily miracle occurred—the work got done, albeit marginally, and only with his father's help. His studying consisted only of aimless reading of the chapter. The light didn't go out until 10:45. Scott's eyelids would need toothpicks the next day.

Scott didn't stand a chance on that test. He hadn't paid enough attention in class, didn't study well, and was fatigued and nervous because he wasn't prepared. Besides, he had poor test-taking skills. By virtue of his intelligence, Scott scraped out a C.

Scott was bright enough to be an A or B student but usually got C's because he didn't know *how* to be a student. The schools should, but too often don't, teach kids how. That leaves you, the parent, to do the job. Start by choosing just one of the following skills, the one that seems most important for your child to learn.

CHAPTER FOUR

How to Help Your Child Care More about School Books than School Clothes

When we were in school, the predominant attitude toward school and teachers was fear. While this eliminated many of the discipline problems that plague today's schools, the students often paid a price. Our friend Debbie told us about an incident that happened to her in the seventh grade:

> Debbie needed to use the bathroom during a test and raised her hand to tell the teacher. He said, "No questions during a test," and motioned her hand down. Afraid to argue, she said nothing. A few minutes later, the need had grown more urgent and she had to raise her hand again, with the same result. Still, she was afraid to say anything. Shortly thereafter, a nearby classmate pointed to a small puddle on the floor and loudly asked where it came from. Poor Debbie ignored him but had to rise from her seat when the bell rang with a large, all too visible stain on her skirt.

Clearly, abject terror is not the attitude we want to instill in our children. Healthy respect tempered with the knowledge that the teacher is human will suffice.

Can you instill in your child a healthy respect for school and teacher? It's not easy; changing attitudes is no mean feat. A manufacturer spends millions just to change the consumer's attitude toward his toilet paper. Psychoanalysts put patients on the couch for years trying to change their attitudes toward their mothers. Your child's attitudes toward education may already be well established, and, like a clump of bamboo, tough to uproot. But since your child's attitude toward education so vitally affects his school success, it's worth making an effort.

Actions Speak Louder Than Words

Probably the most important thing you can do to instill respect for teacher, school, and learning is to show, not just tell, your child that you respect them yourself. No matter how often you tell your child to respect the teacher, if your child senses you don't, she will think, "If Mom thinks Mrs. Gertz is a turkey, then she probably is."

You might ask yourself the following questions to assess how much respect you're showing toward school, teachers, and learning:

- How do you listen to your child talk about school? Is your usual response to his tales, "Uh-huh"?

- How often do you ask your child about school in more detail than, "How was school today?" "Fine, mom." "That's good"?

- How much care do you take in looking at his schoolwork? Do you usually just give a perfunctory glance and a quick "that's nice"?

- Do you try to note the positive things about school while minimizing the negative? Every "Gee, you're really learning a lot this year," and "That is a valuable assignment," makes a difference. Sometimes, it takes some effort. For example, if your child has to define some obscure words, instead of saying, "I don't know why your teacher is making you learn those," you might say, "Wow! You're learning something that most adults don't know."

- Do you, at least occasionally, check his homework?

- Do you encourage learning-oriented recreation; for example, reading aloud regularly to your child even at the higher grade levels rather than permitting nonstop television?

- Do *you* read? Children imitate their parents.

- Do you take your children to the library or encourage them to use it?

- How much do you use the library?

- Do you demonstrate the pleasures of learning by pointing out interesting things while walking, driving, exploring museums, or even your own backyard?

- How do you react to a teacher's request for a conference? Are you more likely to say, "Good; I've been looking forward to chatting with your teacher," or "Doesn't she realize I'll have to take time off."?

- If your child came home from school and said, "My teacher called me 'stupid' in front of the whole class," would you assume the teacher has erred or would you ask your child for the details surrounding the incident? Perhaps what happened was that your child hit a classmate and the teacher said, "That was a stupid thing to do."

While your actions are most important, overtly stating your case can't hurt. Here's one parent's version:

Try to treat your teacher as you would me. That means following her instructions even when you don't want to. Usually the teacher has good reasons, even if you don't understand them. Just do what she says, and if you think she was wrong, tell me about it at home and we'll discuss it.

In a sense, this parent is preaching blind conformity, but having seen the costs of nonconformity in schools, we suspect that school is probably not the best place to teach your child to question authority.

Another lecture deals with the complaining student:

Let's say you're right: your teacher is terrible and the work is boring. But complaining and procrastinating will only make your job harder, probably lower your grades and how much you learn. In the long run, you'll be happier if you just decide to make the work as pleasurable as possible and get it done.

Even when a teacher errs, you can react so your child's respect for the teacher remains intact—you needn't immediately demand an apology from the teacher or run to the principal. A parent describes her daughter's ESP incident:

> When Jessica was in the third grade, her class was studying ESP. One child was sent out of the room while the rest of the class concentrated on "beaming" a three-part message to her: a color, a television show, and a comic book. The person outside tried to receive the beam. Several children had already been outside and tried in vain to guess.
>
> However, when it was Jessica's turn to go out, the teacher decided to play a joke on her. She told the class, 'When she comes in, whatever she guesses, tell her she's right, so she'll think she has ESP.' So when Jessica said, "Purple, L.A. Law, and Spider Man," the class oohed and ahhed in amazement. Jessica was in heaven. She had ESP!
>
> The teacher, I can't imagine why, never told her it was a joke. Poor Jessica came home thrilled with her new "power." It wasn't until the next day that her classmates told her of the put-on. Needless to say, she was crushed as was her trust in her teacher.
>
> I was pretty angry. Fortunately, I followed my rule for when I'm mad: do nothing for twenty-four hours. When I calmed down, I did what I think was the right thing. I wrote the following note to her teacher which I also read to Jessica:

Dear Miss Simpson,
Jessica told me about the ESP "joke,"
that you realized you made a mistake,
and have apologized. Thank you for
that. I told Jessica that teachers,
like all of us, make mistakes, even
serious ones, and unless they occur too
often, deserve to be forgiven. She agreed.
Jessica has enjoyed having you as her
teacher and we look forward to
continued success.
                    Sincerely,
                      Susan White

For the rest of the year, Miss Simpson bent over backwards to be kind to Jessica. In addition, Jessica learned a lesson in forgiveness which enabled her to get along well with Miss Simpson for the rest of the year. Ironically, I think the incident and its aftermath increased her respect for Miss Simpson and for school in general.

A child can only have a good attitude toward school if he believes he can succeed. You can foster this self-confidence by giving your child tasks at home he can succeed at, and praising him when he does succeed. Also try to praise the good things you see in his schoolwork and criticize sparingly. Remember that for most children, school is often a trying experience; a child needs all the encouragement he can get.

For most children, verbal encouragement is enough. Giving tangible rewards for good school performance is unnecessary, indeed undesirable, since they can make children care only about the rewards, not the learning.

But a small percentage of children will only respond to tangible consequences: a chocolate truffle if they finish their homework, no Nintendo if they don't. It's probably better to have a child motivated by tangibles than not motivated at all. After all, how many adults would work if they didn't get paid? But there are some important do's and don'ts of reward systems. Here's an example of the don'ts:

Randy had been averaging C's on his math tests, largely due to lack of effort. His father approached Randy with the following offer: "Get an A on your report card in math and I'll buy you a new bicycle."

For a number of reasons, this plan probably won't help Randy improve:

- Randy will have to sustain good performance for much too long before earning his reward. Especially when just starting a reward system, a child needs to earn a reward quickly or he loses interest.

- The goal of improving from a C to an A on his report card is too difficult. The goal should be one that the child will probably reach if he gives a reasonable effort.

- Both the goal and the reward were chosen by the parent. A reward system can only work if the student agrees both that the goal is important and realistic and the reward worthwhile.

- There was no negative consequence associated with not achieving the goal. Research has demonstrated that the most effective reward systems both provide a reward for achieving the goal and take away a privilege for not achieving it. However, it's important to note that corporal punishment, long-term grounding, or other severe punishments usually cause more problems than they solve.

Here's an example of a more effective reward system. Like Randy, Patrick has been averaging C's on his math tests, largely due to lack of effort. Patrick and his mother discuss the problem and agree that getting at least a B on math tests is an important yet realistic goal. At Patrick's suggestion, his mother agrees to let him stay up one night to watch "Saturday Night Live" if he gets

61

a B or better on his next math test. If he gets a C or worse, there's no television that night and, instead, he has to do math problems for at least a half hour.

Putting the agreement in writing seems to encourage both parties to complete their ends of the bargain. A written contract is also a useful reminder that the agreement exists and what the terms are. Be sure to pay off if your child does what was contracted for, and mete out the negative consequence if he doesn't.

BE CAREFUL: Make sure your child doesn't turn into a reward junkie, someone who requires a tangible reward for doing nearly everything. You can avoid addicting your child by telling him at the outset that a reward is merely a temporary aid to get him on the right track. Also, make it increasingly difficult to get a reward. For example, if your child has been getting C's on his math tests, you might reward him once or twice for getting a B, then require an A. If he gets a few A's, explain that he's shown himself that he can do it and now the challenge is to see if he can continue without the crutch of a reward. Then substitute praise for the tangible reward.

We've discussed how to make your child want to succeed in school. But your child also needs to learn how to deal with failure, since all students fail at one time or another—fail to understand a lesson, fail a test, fail in a social situation, maybe even fail to be promoted to the next grade.

Before a failure even occurs, let your child know that you're aware that everyone fails occasionally and that he can count on your love and support in failure as well as in success. His assurance that your love and respect won't be jeopardized makes him more likely to confide in you when things don't go well.

After a failure, you may first need to console him with hugs and words of support. Then, help turn the failure into a learning experience by discussing what he can do to improve. Try to let the suggestions come from your child—we're all more likely to implement our own ideas. This is particularly true if the idea is to "try harder."

This contract is between _____ (student)

and _____ (teacher, friend, other)

Date: from _____ to _____
                  (this date)   (contract expiration)

Following are the terms of the contract:

_____ (student) will _____

_____

_____

_____

_____ (teacher, friend, other) will _____

_____

_____

When this contract is completed, the contractee will be able to _____

_____

_____

_____

_____

_____

_____   _____
Contractee   Contractor

_____
Witness

This contract may be
terminated by agreement of
parties signing this contract.
New contract(s) may be
negotiated by the same
parties.

OFFICIAL SEAL

Some children believe they can't succeed in school either because they've done poorly in the past, think they're stupid, or believe the teacher doesn't like them. These children often reject the school system to protect their egos. They rationalize, "I could do well if I wanted to, but school is stupid. It's not worth the effort."

If this sounds like your child, try to rid him of these untruths, since they can become self-fulfilling prophecies. He needs to know that most children can achieve reasonable success in school if they have a good attitude (assuming they're in a decent school with a decent teacher). We've seen so many children of mediocre intelligence do just fine in school because of their positive attitudes.

We've discussed a number of ways to help your child develop positive attitudes toward school. No parent always practices them, including us. But your efforts will help your child develop more positive attitudes toward school and teachers.

Helping your child improve his attitude toward school is probably the most difficult thing we ask you to do in this book. While it *is* important, don't be discouraged if you never quite win the battle. More than one successful adult was pulled through school kicking and screaming. Take heart. We focus on other important, but easier-to-tackle skills in the next chapter.

CHAPTER FIVE

A Day in the Life of a Successful Student: Before Class

Minimizing Morning Madness

Many kids have two strikes against them before ever reaching the schoolhouse gate. One of my students told me about a particularly rough morning. Does any of this sound familiar?

"Wake up, Allan," his mother called, "Time to get up!" Allan lifted his head, but surrendered to the grogginess and collapsed again. Twenty minutes later, he awoke to an adrenaline rush, "Oh no, I'm late again! I'll just get dressed real fast and skip brushing my teeth." His shirt didn't quite match his pants and his breath offended, but at least he'd have time for breakfast . . . until he reminded himself of the form his mother had to sign. Where is it? I had it yesterday." Finding it took care of breakfast time.

He was relieved to plop down on the school bus seat, but the relief was short-lived. He realized he had left his math book on the dining room table. "God! I'm always forgetting something. The teacher is going to kill me. Again. I have a headache." Thirty minutes with forty loud school bus riders didn't do much to help. When Allan arrived at school, he felt like he had already put in a full day.

Even if Allan was otherwise a fine student, he was unlikely to thrive in school that day because of morning madness. Allan was probably not the only one with a headache that morning. A child's ineffective morning routine usually means that Mom or

Dad, themselves busy in the morning, have to shake their child awake, find his missing whatever, and make his breakfast.

The steps that contribute to a smooth morning may seem obvious, yet many otherwise good students don't do them, so they're worth pointing out. (Of course, you yourself never rush in the morning!) If your child's morning routine isn't what you'd like, you may find some of the following ideas useful:

Starting right at the beginning, your child needs a reliable system for wake-up. Teach him to use an alarm clock or clock radio—you'll appreciate not having to rouse him each morning. Besides, an alarm clock is more persistent than most parents want to be.

Your child should experiment with different wake-up times until he finds one that allows enough time for the inevitable unexpected. Better to have a few extra minutes than to frantically scramble to make it to school on time.

Be sure he allows plenty of time to get dressed and perform needed ablutions. The child who is so rushed that he dresses sloppily or doesn't brush his teeth will pay a price in his relationships with peers and teachers.

To save time in the morning, some children choose their clothing the night before, but, too often, lose time because morning brings a change in weather conditions or preference. Many children will find that clothing selection should be left as a morning activity.

A word about clothing selection. Everyone, especially a child, tends to judge people on their appearance. We've seen nice kids ostracized by their peers just because of their clothing. For example, Ann's mother was proud of all the clothes she made for her daughter. But they usually were out of style or didn't fit quite right. Despite Ann's protestations, her mother insisted that she wear them. Ann had few friends, and when I asked one of her classmates why, she said, "Ann's sort of weird. You oughtta see her clothes." We're as concerned as any parent about our daughter being too clothes conscious, but we think it important that a child's clothes fit well and are reasonably stylish.

It's easier to recommend than enforce, but parents should retain final say about clothing and makeup because children are often type-cast by their appearance. A child who dresses "punk" or "trampy" tends to be rejected by all except punks or tramps. Teachers may not be above such judgements either.

Many children skip a step between dressing and leaving for school—breakfast. The old adage that breakfast is the most important meal of the day is certainly true for kids. Skipping breakfast makes it likely that lunch, even if it's only school cuisine, will be uppermost in your child's mind for part of the morning. If he doesn't do it already, you may want to teach your child how to make his own breakfast. Something simple like cereal will do.

Your child should make a habit of using the bathroom just before leaving for school. Most children don't like to use the school bathroom. Some even prefer to remain uncomfortable rather than use it.

Your child should have a specific place for the things he takes to school. Ideally, it should be a place he must pass just before leaving; for example, a table near the front door.

Finally, try to minimize your child's commute time to school. A long or noisy commute can take a lot out of him. You may want to investigate a carpool, public transportation, a different walking route, etc.

How to Help Your Child
Become a Recess Success

Many adults have jobs that are less than rewarding. Sometimes, their main source of morale is break time: the juicy gossip over coffee, going shopping with a coworker during lunch, joining the company bowling league, flirting, whatever. Without these, many people's willingness to work might wane.

Children are no different. School usually requires a lot of work that isn't always enjoyable. So, unless your child really loves schoolwork, he may, like adults, need enjoyable break time—recess—to keep his morale up. Without it, like an adult, his willingness to do the work might wane.

Some kids have a wonderful time during recess. For them, recess is a revitalizer that sustains them through good times and bad in the classroom, giving them the emotional reserve to keep plugging until that next recess. But, for other kids, recess is no happier than class time; remember how Scott spent recess wan-

67

dering around? More children than one might think avoid recess completely by spending it in the library or helping the teacher or custodian clean up. These kids don't have the prospect of a happy recess to keep their morale up in class.

It's hard to do well if you can't concentrate in class. Some kids, mainly boys, find concentration particularly difficult. In the old days, these kids were just called "active" and were accepted by teachers as part of the job. But today, active kids can get a pseudomedical label (hyperactive) and even a thrice daily dose of Ritalin, a drug that often benefits the teacher more than the child.

Knowing how to make the most of recess can enable the active child to burn off some energy and develop the resolve to sit still until the next recess, the lethargic child to learn the pleasures of activity, the talkative child to get some chatter out of his system, and the quiet child to come out of his shell. For more kids than one might suspect, recess can make the difference between "I like school" and "I hate school," and even between doing well and not doing well.

Some children seem naturally to know how to make the most of recess. This section is for the many kids who don't and whose lack of recess success can affect their school success.

Making Friends

What can a child do to make friends? We asked this question of fifty fifth to tenth-graders who were honor students and were considered popular among their peers. Rebecca's story summarize their answers.

Rebecca said that she learned how to make friends because her Army family relocated so often. Within the first few days at her new school, she picked out a few kids she wanted to get to know, each of whom seemed to act like her, even look like her.

Within a week, she had started conversations with each of them: about a classmate, classroom activity, the teacher, or the homework. She asked an athletic type if she wanted to play basketball. In all her early interactions, she played what the other kids wanted to play, talked about what they wanted to talk about, knowing there was time later for the other kids to accommodate her. Within a month, Rebecca had a network of friends.

Perhaps more important than what Rebecca did was what she didn't do. She knew the things that usually turn prospective friends off: teasing, being too sensitive to teasing, acting aloof, appearing too anxious to make friends (for example, giving gifts as a bribe for friendship), criticizing others, being too serious or too giggly, showing off, acting silly, tough, or weird, dressing unconventionally or otherwise straining to get attention.

Making friends and getting along with others is obviously too complicated to be reduced to a simple formula, but a child without many friends often doesn't even know where to begin. Rebecca's way, the way recommended by the fifty popular honor students we surveyed, can offer a direction.

The Recess Olympics

It's a miracle. By the sixth grade, most boys, even the weakest students, know the basic rules of basketball, football, softball and lesser-known games. That in itself would be impressive. since even the basic rules are complicated. But the miracle is that they know not the widely published official rules, but the vastly different schoolyard rules, which rarely see the printed page.

This miracle escapes many girls and some boys, leaving them wondering how everyone else seemed to learn. These unfortunates are usually exiled to way-outfield or to some other role in which they never touch the ball. Understandably, they get bored and take an early retirement from sports.

There are many reasons why even nonathletes should know the basics of the most popular schoolyard games:

- Playing can be fun, in and out of school.

- Playing can cure the classroom blues and renew your child's willingness to give his best in school.

- Playing helps kids burn off energy which, if pent up, can make concentrating in the classroom difficult.

- Knowing the basics can enable even nonathletes to play without incurring the hotshots' wrath.

- These games are mainstays of the ever-required physical education classes.

- Outside of school, throughout adulthood, baseball, football, and basketball are key parts of even the nonathlete's life. It's no fun going to the homecoming game if you have no idea what's going on after the cheerleaders leave the field.

To these ends, you and your child might wish to consult an encyclopedia entry on the game of interest, or a guide to schoolyard games such as:

Knapp, M. & P. Knapp, *One Potato, Two Potato: The Secret Education of American Children.* New York, Norton, 1976

Sutton-Smith, B. *Handbook of Children's Folklore.* Washington, D.C.: Smithsonian, 1986.

This chapter has discussed the preliminaries. In the next chapter, we offer tips for winning *in* the classroom the main event.

CHAPTER SIX

A Day in the Life of a Successful Student: The School Hours

You wouldn't think Matt was much of a student. Many concepts require an explanation, or three. As soon as two snowflakes hit the ground, Matt starts praying they'll close the schools.

Yet Matt is an A/B student because he knows the art of being a student. This chapter shows how you can teach this art to your child. Knowing how to be a self-sufficient student is especially vital in the often sink-or-swim large public schools, and is a key to school success, public or private.

Don't try to tackle all the techniques at once. You might just peruse the headings and start by choosing one that you think would particularly benefit your child.

The Art of Paying Attention

Everyone knows it's important to pay attention in class. You can only learn if you're paying attention, and an attentive face is a certain teacher-pleaser. From the nonacademic child's perspective, paying attention actually makes the time go faster. Time never passes as slowly as when you're waiting for it to pass. But everyone also knows that paying attention can be difficult at times, if not downright impossible. Think about some classes or meetings you've attended.

There are no magic cures, certainly none that will reliably take a teenager's mind off a cute classmate or that big game. But there are some techniques that often can help:

- Consciously try to avoid being turned off by a teacher with a poor delivery—learn what he's saying regardless of how he says it,

- Participate: make comments, ask and answer questions, take notes.

- Give yourself a reason to pay attention. Some possible ones are: because the material is important to know for real life, because there will be a test on it, because the teacher will be mad if I don't pay attention, because Mom will be happy if I can tell her what I learned in school today,

- If there's a choice, sit near the teacher and a well-behaved, good student,

- Ask yourself questions as the lesson proceeds: "What's the main idea of what he's saying?" "Where does this fit in the teacher's outline of the lesson?"

- Sit up straight, take a deep breath, and look the teacher right in the eye,

When It's Most Important to Pay Attention

The above suggestions may help, but let's face it, no one, not even we mature adults, can pay attention 100 percent of the time. Can we realistically expect kids to? Perhaps the best we can hope for is that they'll choose wisely when not to pay attention. Peter's choices were less than judicious:

After Mr. Jones had just assigned the homework, Peter, who had been daydreaming, asked, "What's the homework?" Mr. Jones's blood pressure went up, Peter's grade went down.

Mr. Jones was teaching a lesson that obviously took a lot of time to prepare and saw Peter reading a comic book. Mr. Jones's eyes rolled up. Peter's grade went down.

While reexplaining a math concept, Mr. Jones saw Peter passing a note to a child who particularly needed the extra instruction. Mr. Jones got fed up, Peter's grade went down.

There are certain times when paying attention is particularly important:

- **At the beginning of a lesson or activity.** Why? Because important material is usually covered at the beginning: the objectives of the lesson, how the lesson is related to previous learning, directions for an activity. Not paying attention at the beginning often results in being lost from then on.

- **When the teacher seems to be emphasizing a point.** How can you tell? Tip-offs include when the teacher slows his rate of speech, speaks louder, writes something on the board, spends a lot of time on one point, or uses phrases that let you know he's saying something important: "the main point is," "therefore," "to summarize," "let me make this clear," "on the test I might ask you."

- **When directions are being given.** While this may seem obvious, many students don't pay attention at this crucial time.

- **During summaries.** At the end of most lessons and sometimes during, the teacher reviews the main points.

- **At the end of a lesson.** In addition to giving a summary of key points, the teacher usually gives the directions for the next activity.

- **At the beginning and end of the period or day.** Teachers tend to save important announcements for these times.

- **When there is a visitor in the room, particularly an adult.** Why? Because a class that is paying attention reflects positively on the teacher. I practically glowed when my students performed well during a principal's visit to my classroom.

When Paying Attention Isn't So Important

Our children are unlikely to strive to concentrate harder if, like the old schoolmarm, we admonish them to *always* pay attention. They will probably marvel at how delusional we are. We stand a better chance of having an effect if we're realistic—acknowledge that even the best students occasionally pass a note to a friend, and let them know the best times to do it.

Paying attention isn't so important when a child wouldn't miss, or cause others to miss, important learning and when it wouldn't annoy the teacher. Such times exist, and if your child knows they exist, he may be able to postpone going off-task until then. When are these times?

- **During independent seatwork.** During this time, students are usually asked to do written work at their own pace. Teachers usually aren't very concerned if a child briefly goes off-task during seatwork because he can probably still get his work done in time, isn't missing any of the teacher's words of wisdom, and any whispering doesn't distract the teacher as it might if he were teaching a lesson. Of course, it's best to first finish the work and then kick back as time permits.

- **At other times when the teacher is not expecting students to pay direct attention to him.** Such times include: the transition time between activities (for example, when one set of books is being collected and another distributed), when the teacher is reading a message to himself from the office, and when he's doing any last minute preparation for a lesson. Most teachers don't mind a little whispering while the class is waiting for him.

- **At the very beginning or end of a class period** (with some teachers). Some teachers don't actually start class until a few minutes after the period has officially begun. Some end a few minutes before it officially ends. While such time-wasting is poor teaching practice, it nonetheless offers students a safe time to relax.

The preceding guidelines are applicable to many, but not all, classrooms. Whispering while the teacher takes attendance may be fine in most classrooms, but a teacher's peeve in your child's class. So, early in each school year, your child should learn the do's and don'ts of his classroom.

Taking Notes

After the first few years of school, the teachers get tougher. They want proof that the students have been paying attention—a high test score. The good note taker has a leg up. How can your child be a good note taker without having to be a stenographer?

Pity the poor "tape recorder," the student who tries to scribble down everything the teacher says. He usually leaves class drained, with a mass of marginally legible notes to learn, essentially for the first time, since he was too busy "tape recording" when he was supposed to be learning. Typically the notes don't get looked at until the night before the test, by which time he is overwhelmed both by their quantity and by his lack of understanding of them.

In contrast, consider the "distiller," the good note taker. Ready for some good news? The best note takers write fairly little, jotting down only the phrases (never whole sentences) that summarize the teacher's major points and a few important specifics. This gives them the time to think about what the teacher is saying and makes it easy to keep their notes legible. They mark particularly important points by starring, underlining, or highlighting with yellow marker and leave class having already learned much of the material and with a manageable amount of notes to review.

The good note taker goes on to solidify his learning by, *that day*, rereading his notes, making additions as needed, and making sure it all makes sense. If he has a question, he makes a note to ask it the next day. Then, the night before the test, he usually only needs to do a brief general review and then focus on any weak spots. No cramming, and probably a good test score.

Answering Questions

Another key to thriving in school is knowing when and how to respond to the teacher's questions. Answering a question is one of the few times your child gets to interact one-to-one with the teacher. He should make the most of it.

The good student raises his hand frequently, any time he has some idea of the answer. A student with his hand up is learning, since he can't help but think about the question. Also teachers appreciate students whose hands always seem to be raised; it's an easy way to make points with the teacher.

When called on, your child should consciously try to express his thoughts clearly, a difficult task for most children and many adults, but a goal worth working toward. He should also keep answers concise—no one likes the student who takes three paragraphs to cover what could be said in one sentence.

How to Know the Answer When Called On

It's no fun getting called on when you don't know the answer, but there's a secret to avoiding it. Your child will be called on frequently if he raises his hand each time he has some idea of the answer. So, when the teacher asks a question he can't answer, he can keep his hand down and the teacher will probably call on someone who hasn't been answering questions so often. Using this technique, your child will know the answer most times he's called on, thus showing his best side to the teacher and the class and avoiding any embarrassment in having to say, "I dunno."

Nonetheless, your child will undoubtedly be called on occasionally when he's not prepared to answer the questions. These times, while uncomfortable, can offer a learning opportunity if he tries to grapple with the question rather than getting flustered, shrugging his shoulders, or muttering "I dunno," which the teacher may interpret as inattention or indifference. Most teachers appreciate the effort even if the response is feeble, especially if no one else is raising his hand. The good teacher will even give a custom-tailored follow-up based on the student's response:

Mrs. Beder asked Mary, "Why does a piccolo make a higher sound than a flute?" Mary shrugged her shoulders. Mrs. Beder then asked Jill who also didn't know, but mustered up a response, "Well, the piccolo is shorter. Does that have anything to do with it?" "Yes it does. Remember what we learned yesterday about the difference between sound waves of high and low pitches? Does that give you a hint?" "Yes. I guess the sound waves vibrate faster in the piccolo because they travel a shorter distance before hitting the walls of the piccolo."

Jill's first response, though inadequate, encouraged Mrs. Beder to lead her to the correct answer, especially since she ended her response with a question. Though Mary and the other students may also have profited from the explanation, Jill will probably understand and remember it better. Also, even though neither Mary nor Jill knew the answer, Mrs. Beder is probably left with a positive thought about Jill and a negative one about Mary.

If your child draws a complete blank when called on, rather than just sitting there, it's better to say, "I'm really not sure."

That, at least, gives the appearance of having tried. It may even elicit a hint from the teacher.

Asking Questions

Many students (even college students) feel shy about asking the teacher a question, either because they're afraid the teacher will think they're dumb or because they don't like to be the focus of attention.

But students who thrive in school ask lots of questions, one of the most important of which is, "Can you explain that again?" Rather than thinking that such questions are dumb, most teachers are pleased to answer them and view them as signs of an interested student. Other students, reluctant to ask for a second explanation, are usually glad someone else was brave enough to ask.

Asking for a second explanation can keep a child from getting lost or from doing an assignment incorrectly. I've seen students, even at the college level, who did poorly on assignments simply because they didn't understand the assignment, but didn't ask for clarification.

Even more important is asking for help with an ongoing problem, for example, with a classmate, seat location, or inappropriate level of work. When I was in the ninth grade, I really struggled in algebra but was too shy to ask for help, ever, even though I was getting very low grades. I spent much of that year being alternately sad and scared about doing so poorly. Perhaps the school should have been more alert to the problem, especially because my math grade had dropped so precipitously, but it's easy for a school problem to go unnoticed in the large classes of public schools.

That's why children, even young ones, should learn to take some responsibility for their own education and ask the teacher for help when there's an ongoing problem. Some of the most difficult but most potentially beneficial words a child can say to a teacher are, "I'm having a problem with _____. Can you help me?"

There's a right and wrong time to ask questions. Some kids simply blurt out their questions as soon as they enter consciousness and are surprised when the teacher says, "No questions.

Later." That is the child who goes home and complains, "Mommy, my teacher is mean. She won't even answer my questions." While teachers generally welcome questions, they'd rather not answer one when they're preoccupied. How would you feel as a teacher, if you were trying to calm a sobbing child and little Johnny asks, "Can you help me with problem 43?" Before asking a question, kids should ask themselves whether this is a good time to ask. Before or after class is a possibility, especially if it's a serious problem. The teacher may have more time to listen and the child won't have to discuss a problem in front of his classmates.

Making Comments

To learn, a student must be actively involved. We've already covered three ways he can do this, by paying attention, asking questions, and answering questions. Contributing comments to class discussion is a fourth. In addition to keeping a student actively involved, it enables a child to get the teacher's reaction to his thoughts. From the nonacademic child's perspective, participating is another easy way to make points with the teacher.

But as with questions, some students are afraid to make comments for fear of appearing dumb. Indeed, sometimes their fears are justified. Take the following example in which the class is looking at slides of sixteenth-century European paintings and discussing what they suggest about life in that age. One child had just made the perceptive observation, "The pictures show only very rich and very poor people. There probably wasn't much of a middle class." Before the teacher could even compliment Kelly, Ann blurted out, "When's our museum trip?"

Some children, especially at the elementary school level, have a knack of coming up with such lines. But they soon get embarrassed by all the rolled eyes, groans, and laughter and eventually stop participating, a pattern that may be hard to break. Here are five rules for groan-free participation:

1. Actively listen to the discussion before commenting.

2. Try not to repeat what was already said.

3. Confine comments to the topic at hand.

4. Keep comments short—the meat of most ideas can usually be said in a few sentences or less.

5. Make two to three comments per hour of discussion, given an average-size classroom. Six per hour and you're probably too dominating. One or more per hour and you're probably not active enough.

Written Work

Students spend much time writing in school, doing compositions, worksheets, and reports. So to thrive in school, your child must do well on written work.

While being a Hemingway helps, many average writers get good grades on written work just by paying close attention to the superficialities: neatness, following directions on headings, format, and length, and wrapping work in fancy covers. These are always somewhat important but are crucial in school for many reasons. We list quite a few of them in hope of convincing your child of the importance of form:

- Grading written work is often subjective, so it's tempting for a teacher, if only subconsciously, to give weight to objective characteristics like neatness.

- Teachers always have many papers to grade, causing much eyestrain. When they come to a neat paper, there is a feeling that here they can relax. There is unconsciously a good feeling toward the paper and its author. When they come to an illegible, cramped paper, there is, conversely, an unconscious tension, a feeling of "here we go up the hill again," which may spill over into the grade.

- Especially at the lower grade levels, teachers grade, in part, on effort. Effort readily manifests itself in neatness and plastic covers.

- Your child gets most of his feedback in school from the teacher's comments on his written work. So, it's important that his papers be carefully read and commented on. Teachers try to give all papers equal attention, but on seeing a paper that looks carelessly done, a teacher can think again unconsciously, "If he wasn't concerned enough to even take care of the superficial things, then why should I bother to read his paper carefully? I have stacks more to read from kids who care about their work."

- If the teacher wants to give feedback, a sloppy paper can make it impossible. Consider, for example, the situation in which a child gets an item wrong on a math test. If the teacher can't decipher the work leading to an incorrect answer, he can do no more than to mark it wrong. If the work were legible, he could, for example, circle the exact place where the student made an error and perhaps give partial credit for the answer.

- Neatness and following directions are necessary to succeed in our society so your child should work toward achieving them.

- From the nonacademic child's perspective, packaging the product well is an easy way to higher grades.

Paper Packaging Tips

In terms of the grade, it's safest to make written work approximately the assigned length. Beyond being safe, attempting to cover the material in a specified space is a useful exercise. It's next safest to make it a little longer. Extra length is often interpreted as a sign of industry. But check that the content couldn't be covered within the assigned limit. It usually can. Least safe is to write a paper much shorter than the specified length. Unless the work is of unimpeachable quality, a teacher may interpret a short paper as a sign of indolence. On the other hand, learning to say a lot in a short space is a worthwhile goal and may justify the risk of a lower grade.

Thanks to the wonders of modern technology, children now have some easy routes to impressive looking papers. First and most potent is the word processor, which we've found indispensable in writing this book. If you can afford one (these days, an "obsolete" model can be the best value for the dollar—you can get one for about $700, complete with printer), it's worth the money and the time it takes for your child to learn to use it. Many word-processing programs are fairly easy for children to learn.

While learning to type is no mean feat, it is and will continue to be, a vital skill, so learning will be worth the effort. Fortunately, there are good computer programs for learning to type, for example, "Mavis Beacon Teaches Typing" or "Typing Tutor."

With a word processor, all papers come out typed, free of corrections. More importantly, the writer can turn out a better product with less effort. Let's say that in proofreading a paper, you noticed that it would make more sense to reverse the order of two paragraphs. If you wrote the paper on a word processor— a few seconds, and voilá, you have a perfectly neat paper with the change made. If the paper were written on a typewriter or by hand, you would be faced with a sloppy cut-and-paste job or rewriting the entire page, which could tempt you to leave it as is. More typically, in proofing a paper, you find dozens of changes that could or should be made, all of which are easy to make on a word processor, but sloppy or cumbersome without one.

Next best is typing. Typed papers are not only more legible than handwritten, they also somehow appear to have required more effort. This often translates into a higher grade.

Then, there is the poor man's word processor, the erasable pen. Pencil, while erasable, just isn't as legible. Students should use erasable pen for all their handwritten work if the teacher will allow it. Liquid correction fluids like Liquid Paper can help when you have to use nonerasable pens.

What Goes in the Package

Finally, we come to content. Here are a few tips that can improve the content of most written schoolwork without requiring much extra effort:

- Your child should try to select a topic that, while still within the assigned limits, is something he's interested in. If he's interested in the topic, writing the paper will be less painful. He might choose a topic related to something he already knows a lot about—a person learns most by proceeding from something he already knows. If the assigned limits seem too restrictive, he might ask if he can do a slightly different assignment. Often, a teacher won't mind accommodating, if only because it gets boring reading thirty papers on the same topic.

- Do the expected plus one. This means that your child should carefully do what was assigned, but add one little extra to make his paper stand out from the rest. Imagine how the teacher feels having to read 30 papers (perhaps 150 at the secondary level) on "My Summer Vacation"! Wouldn't you feel positively disposed toward a paper that gave the assignment a little twist? Perhaps your child might do his composition on his fantasy summer vacation. If your child's homework is to see what happens when you put a celery stalk into a glass of water with food coloring, he might try doing it both in warm and cold water to see if there's any difference.

- Your child should go through the following four steps in writing all compositions and reports: 1) Outline (this can be as simple as listing in order the main points he wants to make and then putting them in a few categories; 2) Rough draft; 3) Careful editing; 4) Final draft. (A more detailed procedure is presented in the next chapter.)

- All reports and compositions should have an interesting title, one that is different from anyone else's in the class. For example, the poorest title for a report on one's summer vacation is "My Summer Vacation." Why not "Hot Time in the Heat"?

- On worksheets, your child should write something down for all items unless he's absolutely blank, in which case he should ask for help. Much learning occurs from trying to figure out problems about which he's unsure. Also, complete papers are often viewed as a sign of effort and thus improve report card grades.

- When teachers return corrected written work, most children make the mistake of just looking at the grade. Not examining the teacher's comments is like plugging your ears when the teacher is working one-to-one with you. Try to convince your child to examine all comments and corrections, asking himself, "Do I understand it now?" and, if not, to ask the teacher for clarification. When he gets positive comments, he might try to remember to do more of the same the next time.

The Art of Being Organized

No, it's not hopeless, even if your child's desk is perpetually a tornado of papers, and his most frequent question is, "Where's my _____?"

You may never transform your slob into a neat freak, but you can teach him a few tricks that can enable even a slob to be functionally organized in school. The problem is that many disorganized children aren't particularly interested in becoming more organized. Most of them believe it takes too much effort. A few more sophisticated slobs believe that organization is trivial, the incorrect valuing of form over substance. They don't realize that substance is often affected by organization and that children pay a heavy price for being disorganized in school. Spending a particularly bad twenty minutes with one of my less organized students may convince your free spirit:

"Boys and girls, take out your 'Person I Most Admire' reports. I want you to spend the next twenty minutes on it. Make good use of the note cards you compiled in the library."

Steven was happy; now he'd have a chance to catch up. He eagerly reached for his note cards but could only find three. "Dr. Nemko! Someone took my note cards." (Nineteen minutes left.)

"Steven, I'm sure no one took your note cards. Are you sure you put them in your desk?"

"Yes, I'm sure."

"Okay, Steven, let's look." We emptied his desk and found a comic book, four crumpled worksheets (one, five months old), two sheets covered with doodles (fortunately, no portraits of me), three pencils (without erasers, of course), and a highly incriminating amount of used bubble gum. No note cards. (Fifteen minutes left.)

"Steven, why don't you look in your notebook binder?" He shuffled through all the loose sheets. Some had fallen out because he hadn't used reinforcements, others had never gotten into the binder because he "didn't have time." Finally, about halfway through, he found the rest of the note cards and called out proudly, "I found them, Dr. Nemko!" I mustered a half-hearted, "Good, Steven. Now get busy." (Twelve minutes left.)

Steven was doing his report on Mother Teresa. He knew that the next thing he needed to write on was her experience at the convent. But in looking through his cards, he had written only one sentence. He'd have to go back to the library. (Eight minutes left.)

"Well, Dr. Nemko said we could use some pictures in our report. I'll draw one of Mother Teresa's home." He took out his crayons and drew for a while until (three minutes left) ... "I need raw umber. Mine's missing. Darlene, do you have a raw umber crayon I could borrow?"

"Not for you. You never return things."

"Hey, Miguel! Do you have a raw umber crayon?"

"You promise to return it?"

"Yeah." (Two minutes left.) Two minutes of raw umbering later, I said, "Time for math."

Despite his good intentions, Steven's disorganization doomed him to failure. Fortunately, even scatterbrains can learn to be organized enough to get their schoolwork done without a lot of wasted time and frustration.

Storing Papers

First, your child should know that, unless a teacher requires a different type, the best paper storage system is usually an $8^1/_2$ x 11-inch three-ring binder, especially one with built-in file folders or a clip. If your child thinks binders are for sissies, he can make it more hip by plastering it with pictures of motorcycles, movie stars, or the latest rock group.

As opposed to the spiral notebook, the three-ring binder allows for neat removal and insertion of pages. But it's only neat if you can convince your child to follow a simple ritual: whenever he needs to store paper, he puts reinforcements on it and puts it into the section of the binder for that subject. Any papers he won't need go right in the trash.

File folders or a clip built into the binder are a good place to store papers that need to go home: those A papers to show Mom, the field trip permission slip that must be signed, the specifications for the big assignment. If every child put all homebound papers in a file folder or clip, there would be far fewer zeros for no homework and fewer angry parents scolding, "Why didn't you give me that form?"

One of the most important things to go into the homebound file folder or on the clip is a small memo pad. A child should get into the habit of using a memo pad, not only to list all homework assignments, but also other things to remember: sneakers for gym tomorrow, milk money, etc.

Within the binder rings, your child should have a zipper bag well stocked with erasable pens that work, and erasers. Running out will then be a rare event, making your child more likely to remember to replenish. Also, even though it means more to carry, the binder should have a good supply of paper. Teachers get annoyed with children who are always asking to borrow a pencil or paper.

Perhaps more important than your child organizing his papers and school supplies, is organizing his school *time*. This is often the secret behind children who seem to get all their work done and still have plenty of time for fun. Studies have shown that there is a great deal of dead time in the school day during which a student can get school or homework done. The student who wants time for fun after school gets homework done when finished early with another assignment or while otherwise waiting for the teacher. The obsessive child tries to avoid homework totally, by spending recess in the library or working on the way to or from school.

The successful student also makes the most of time spent working. Adults may know the following rules for efficiency, but many kids don't, especially those that complain about too much homework.

Rule 1: Do the difficult work when you're fresh, the easier work when you're fatigued or don't feel like working but you know you should.

Rule 2: Do the most important things. First; if you can't finish everything, only the least important things will go undone.

Your child should remember that much of the organization for school success occurs outside of school. In the previous chapter, we offered some tips for morning organization. In this chapter, we've offered some for during school. In the next chapter, we'll share some for after school.

Secrets to High Test Scores

It's easy to hate tests. But they have some redeeming qualities. A test is a fairly objective way for teachers to keep score of the school game. Without tests, your child's grades would be more subject to the teacher's biases. Tests also teach: taking and going over the test can be educational.

Like them or not, tests are important. They affect report card grades, can help get your child into the "smart" class, and can make the difference between admission to the college of his choice and the college of their choice.

Just the psychological effects of a good versus a poor test grade can be powerful. Remember how you felt as the teacher was walking up and down the aisles returning the test papers? How did you feel when she smiled at you as she returned your A? Contrast it with how you felt when you saw that D or F. A good test grade usually motivates, a poor one discourages.

Test-taking skills can't turn a C student into a valedictorian, but they can make a difference. Here are some hints for successful test taking to share with your child.

Opening Strategies

Everyone's somewhat nervous at test time. Although too much tension is bad, a bit can provide extra drive to attack the test. The best way to keep from getting too nervous is, unfortunately, not an easy one—be well prepared for the test. In addition, your child should have plenty of writing equipment so he's not begging for an eraser at the last second. He might also take a few deep breaths and stretch, before and during the test.

Before even receiving the test paper, the older child might try to step into the teacher's mind: what did he emphasize in class? How deep an understanding does he expect? What are his biases? Will he be tricky? Keeping the test maker in mind will help your child give the answers the teacher is looking for.

The first thing to do when receiving the test paper is to carefully listen to, or read the directions. The low scorer is often so worried about finishing the test in time that he skims the directions, causing many unnecessary wrong answers. Many students have written four essays when the directions specified choosing three of four.

If there are both short-answer and essay items, the short-answer items should typically be done first, as quickly as possible without sacrificing accuracy. Then your child can figure out how much time to allow for each essay. Also, multiple-choice questions often contain information which can be used in an essay.

Attacking the Test Items

Many students lose points by not reading the question carefully. Each test question should be read as carefully as the directions—the question is the directions for that item. Questions asking for the negative are particularly prone to error; for example, "Which is the least important?" Of course, if your child isn't sure of the directions to an item, he should ask the teacher.

The most important test-taking skill is conquering the tough items. Even the best students encounter many items they're not sure of. Low scorers often get flustered, quickly make a wild guess, and go on. But high scorers know they'll get many of them right if they just spend some extra seconds figuring out a way to make an intelligent rather than a wild guess. This attitude not only improves scores but helps the test-taker to relax and even enjoy the process, thinking of every tough item as a challenge, a puzzle which can often be solved with some ingenuity.

This approach can be particularly fruitful in a multiple-choice test. Slick reached the following item on a science test:

Which is the smallest?

a. a gene   c. a cell

b. a contractile vacuole   d. a chromosome

Slick didn't know the answer but wasn't deterred.

"Okay, are there any choices I'm sure are wrong? Yes. I'm pretty sure the cell is bigger than the rest of them. Well, that uses up all my knowledge. Now, how can I eliminate some of the other choices? I don't know what a contractile vacuole is, but I don't think Mrs. Newhouse ever mentioned contractile vacuole in class, and I don't remember seeing it in the textbook, so I figure that can't be the answer. Now, the choice is between a gene and a chromosome. Well, this test has already had a few questions on chromosomes, and none on genes, so I'm going to go with "a gene."

If your child is still stuck after about thirty seconds, he should make his best guess, put a dot next to the item so he can come back to it if he has time, and go on. An item should rarely be left unanswered—only if the test directions specify a penalty for guessing and your child has absolutely no idea of the answer, unable to eliminate even one choice in a multiple-choice question. Tests like the Scholastic Aptitude Test have a penalty for guessing. Most teacher-made tests do not, except, occasionally, a true/false test.

When I was in the seventh grade, our science teacher told us whenever you are torn between two choices, it is safest to select the answer that is closest to the middle because test makers tend to "hide" the correct response in the middle. Although I'm not sure that his advice has any merit, I always followed it when facing two choices that I could not decide between. It just felt better to have some way of choosing between them.

A key to success on math tests is to avoid carelessness. Here are some common blunders to avoid:

- adding instead of multiplying ($2 \times 3 = 5$)

- forgetting to convert feet to inches

- forgetting to list the unit of measurement (9 inches rather than 9)

- putting the decimal point in the wrong place, or lining up numbers improperly; for example,

$$\begin{array}{r} 427 \\ -38 \\ \hline 47 \end{array}$$

If there's time after finishing all the items, your child should go over the difficult ones he put a dot next to, but only change the original answer if he's quite sure it's wrong. Research indicates that students' first answers tend to be correct.

Essay Tests

The following procedure can help students do well on an essay test even when they're a bit tentative on the content.

First, your child should read all the questions, then begin with the easiest one and work up to the most difficult. There are two reasons for this: first, if he doesn't have time to finish, the hardest will be left undone. Second, doing easier essays often triggers thoughts on the hard ones. Sometimes, a bit of incubation time helps.

Your child should allow more time for the difficult essays. For example, if there are forty minutes to do three essays, two of which he finds easy, he might allow ten minutes for each of the first two, leaving twenty minutes for the difficult one.

If the essay is at all complex, he should first, on scratch paper, list as many points as possible that directly answer the question, using no more than a phrase for each point. If he can't list enough points, he should think of a closely related topic that he can expand upon. Then, the points should be grouped logically—putting a "1" next to each item in the first group he wants to present, a "2" next to each item in the second group, etc. At this point, your child has an outline and can write a well-organized report with less need to revise.

The essay should begin with a brief introductory paragraph summarizing how the question will be addressed. Then, the points from the outline should be explained in order, and in good, clear English.

If indirectly relevant points must be used, he must present a convincing reason for using them. For example, consider a situation in which the question was, "What factors spurred the Industrial Revolution?" The student ran out of factors after listing just one, but he knew much about the cotton gin, so he wrote the following: "Perhaps the impact of this factor can best be appreciated by an example. Take, for instance, the cotton gin."

This approach of using indirectly relevant points will probably yield a better score than if he tried to "pad"—to say his one directly relevant point in as many words as possible. Nonetheless, it is safer to write a slightly longer than a slightly shorter essay.

End the essay with a brief summary and a last sentence, putting the topic in a larger context, perhaps relating it to the past, present, or future. For example, for the question on the Industrial Revolution, one might say, "While we admire the contribution of the Industrial Revolution, we might also consider the price to our environment, a considerable one today, a likely greater one tomorrow."

If there are three minutes left and the entire last (and hardest) essay is still staring your child in the face, he might try writing, "Short of time; please accept outline." and then listing, in phrase outline form, all the points. There's nothing to lose—it was the hardest essay anyway.

If your child isn't a great writer, he may be better off writing each essay as a list of key points. Doing so enables him to make a clear presentation, yet may hide his writing weaknesses.

Finally, your child should know about the following study. Two identical essays were copied by hand, one using perfect handwriting, the other marginally legible. Each version was given to a group of teachers for grading. The highly legible version received significantly higher grades.

Computer-Scored Tests

More test takers than one might imagine lose points because of errors made in transferring their answers to the answer sheet. So, when finishing a computer-scored test, your child should check to see that he put his answers in the right places.

The Scholastic Aptitude Test (or American College Testing Program Examination) is, perhaps, the most important test a college-bound child ever takes. After grade point average, SAT score is often the most important factor in college admissions. What can be done to improve your child's performance?

There's no substitute for ongoing diligence, but a bit of specific test preparation can help: taking the PSAT (Preliminary Scholastic Aptitude Test) as a sophomore in high school and then, a few weeks before taking the SAT, going through one of the commercially available SAT preparation books. For those students more likely to be motivated by a computer than by a book, computer programs are available for about $30, but in substance, they do little more than a book.

The value of a formal SAT preparation course is unclear, but there is some evidence that such a course may help, particularly if a student needs to brush up in math, has a weak vocabulary, or suffers undue test anxiety.

Getting the Test Back

The teacher has just returned the test papers. It's easy to think only about the grade as the teacher is going over the test. But it's worth paying attention to the correct answers, at least for the questions your child got wrong. If your child didn't do well, this is a time to reflect on how to improve. If he did well, it may be time to savor the success a bit.

Common School Problems

At some point in their school careers, most students encounter a problem with another child, with the teacher, or with missing school materials. Knowing how to deal effectively with these problems is another way to help your child thrive, not just survive, in school.

Dealing with Bullies and Other Hazardous Organisms

Learning to deal with day-to-day problems with classmates is part of a child's education. It's a matter of learning good problem solving and communication skills. But, special tactics are often required to deal with problem children. Even the best schools have a few children whose favorite pastime is intimidating others.

Fortunately, your child can do some things to reduce his chances of being the target. Obviously, your child shouldn't hang around with these kids, especially during recess, lunch, and before and after school, when students are least supervised. But when problem children are unavoidable, it's probably best to be mildly cordial: friendly enough not to arouse anger, but not so friendly that they decide to make your child their best friend.

Bullies usually don't strike at random—they tend to pick on kids who themselves are less than angelic. If your child is a frequent target, you can sometimes discover whether he's doing anything to instigate the trouble, by having the teacher meet with Bronco and your child, or by asking a teacher or recess supervisor to watch your child at recess.

91

Occasionally, despite your child's best efforts, he may find himself the object of some monster's scorn. No need to panic, yet.

Imagine yourself as a child at recess one day. Suddenly, the class tough guy, Big Biff, charges at you and from two inches away yells, "Hey, chump! I'm sick of you. Every time I get a question wrong, you just love getting it right and making me look like a fool. Well now I'm gonna redecorate your face."

Here are four possible responses:

1. "The hell with you. I can't help it if you're dumber than I, and everyone else in the class." This response risks dismemberment.

2. "Gee, I'm sorry. I didn't mean to hurt your feelings." [The twerp response.] There's some chance Biff will go for this one, but there's a better chance it will only legitimize his anger and encourage him to redecorate.

3. "Listen. If you don't leave me alone, I'll tell the teacher." Threats often won't work, especially with a Biff. He probably is very familiar with "getting in trouble" and knows that nothing serious ever happens. The threat probably will just get him angrier still, bringing about a face renovation instead of just a redecoration.

4. "Come on, my face is so ugly already, it's not worth redecorating." Children, including Biffs, have told us that humor can often diffuse a Biff, especially if the target makes himself the butt of the humor.

Many bullies like to be mean just for the fun of it. The child who reacts too seriously is asking for more. Bullies can be sadistic, and if they see they're getting to a child, may taunt him more. The response of choice is to try and laugh it off or even to return the teasing jokingly. Getting angry is a fast way to escalate the teasing into a fight.

If a child can't cajole a Biff into relenting, telling the teacher or principal is probably the next step. But, as we said, that can cause more problems with Biff.

Sometimes no pacifist strategy will work. An occasionally worthwhile last resort is to fight it out. While fighting in school cannot heartily be recommended, especially with a Big Biff, I have seen instances when it was the only alternative. Mark had been picked on incessantly by the school's tough guy, let's call him, Bruiser. Each time, Mark reported it to the teacher and Bruiser got punished, ever more severely. Still, he continued to harass Mark. Finally, Mark got fed up and during a recess slugged it out with him. Bruiser got the best of it and Mark ended up with a black eye and a bloody nose. But Bruiser gained respect for Mark's bravery and never bothered him again. Mark always remembered the incident with a certain amount of pride.

Fortunately, Mark had followed three rules for this sort of fight:

1. If a fight is inevitable, don't wait for the other kid to hit you—take him by surprise by hitting him when and where he least expects it;

2. Put all your force into the first blow; don't start with a half-hearted shove; and

3. Aim for a spot that is very vulnerable. The nose is also good.

When There's a Problem with the Teacher

Even the best students occasionally receive a reprimand like, "Stop talking and get back to work." These aren't serious and the teacher forgets them quickly. Usually, the best response is to say nothing and be especially good for awhile.

Unfortunately, some children turn a mild rebuke into a federal case. Especially if they feel wrongly accused, they try to establish their innocence: "I wasn't talking!" This is usually a bad move. The teacher may perceive this child as defiant or even dishonest since he truly believed the child was wrong or he wouldn't have reprimanded him in the first place.

If a child feels unfairly accused or inappropriately treated, he shouldn't argue with the teacher in front of the class, and probably not at all. If he considers it very important, he might politely tell the teacher after class. Then, the teacher may have more time to discuss it, and isn't having his judgement questioned in front of the other students.

Problems with School Equipment

Teachers get justifiably exasperated with having to spend so much time dealing with "lost" textbooks, "missing" paper, and "stolen" pencils. Of course, the best solution is to come to school with all necessary paraphernalia. But, if a child finds himself lacking an item, he should avoid asking the teacher and instead, "borrow" from a usually well-equipped classmate.

Staying after School

Many children come home from school to find themselves with plenty of spare time—time they spend bored, in front of the tube, or even getting in trouble. Unless your child's schedule is already overloaded, you might encourage him to join an after-school club or activity. Some schools have many to choose from: a school newspaper, yearbook committee, sports, debating teams, Model United Nations, La Organización de Latinos Americanos, etc.

Staying after school to help a teacher can offer special benefits. The teacher may view it as a favor, and the child will have the rare opportunity to spend some good one-on-one time with the teacher. It's a good way to encourage a teacher to take a special interest in your child.

Each year, a few days before school begins, our daughter used to help her former first grade teacher prepare for the first day. Doing this allowed her to spend some one-on-one time with a cherished teacher, and made her feel like a part of the school system, in turn, enhancing her overall attitude toward her education.

Leaving School

How many times have you heard, "I left my _____ at school."? Just before leaving school each afternoon, the good student makes sure he has everything he needs to take home—texts, assignments, forms, graded work to show Mom and Dad, the construction paper he needs for his report, the phone number of a classmate who can help with the math he didn't understand.

The student who has thrived in school leaves feeling very different from one who has just survived. The mere survivor is usually drained from failure after failure, even at recess. He didn't pay attention when it was important to, which may have caused poor work or the teacher's ire. He rarely participated in class discussions, so he always felt bored. He was further discouraged by low grades, caused largely by his disorganization, poor note taking and test taking skills, and not knowing how to do well on written work. He often leaves school dreading the thought of homework and of returning to school the next morning.

In contrast, the successful student usually leaves school feeling satisfied. He has achieved a measure of success, not because he worked harder, but because he worked smarter. The successful student makes life still easier on himself by judicious use of after school time, the topic of the next chapter.

CHAPTER SEVEN

A Day in the Life
of a Successful Student:
After School

When we were kids, it felt so good to get home after school—milk, cookies, and a cheery mother to hear about our day. Thus rejuvenated, we could usually face our homework, Mom helping us through the rough spots. The smells, the sounds, the fact of Mom making dinner dulled the pain of homework.

For our daughter, this is but a fantasy. When she was younger, she went to an after-school child care center. Now she usually comes home to an empty house, and, when we get home, we're not June and Ward Cleaver; we're tired, sometimes irritable, and grateful when she can do her homework by herself.

Our family's situation is not rare. Twenty years ago, a child would be pitied if he came home after school to an empty house. Now, latchkey children are a fact of life.

So, today's children need to know how to get their homework done well, without parental assistance, and still have time for fun. This chapter explains how to teach this to your child, how to recognize if your child really needs your help with homework, and how to provide it quickly and without tears.

Don't try to teach your child all the skills in this chapter at once. You might just choose one idea that you think might especially help your child. Most children in the early grades have little homework, so most of the techniques in this chapter will become increasingly useful in upper grades.

How Your Child Can Finish His Homework and Still Have Time For Fun

Are You Interfering?

"Mom, I get so much homework, I never have time for fun." Often the problem is not too much homework, but overscheduling and poor use of time. Overscheduling may be the parent's fault. Many parents round out their children's education with after-school activities: household responsibilities, instruction in music, sports, dancing, and religion. These are fine in moderation, but being a student is usually a full-time job, so kids can suffer if their parents overschedule them.

A particular bugaboo of ours is music lessons, a prodigious time-consumer. Many parents feel that their child should learn to play an instrument. Often they go to considerable expense and inconvenience to provide private lessons while their children show their gratitude by complaining constantly about practicing. These parents don't relent for a few years despite clear evidence of little talent and less enjoyment being derived. (Of course, for the truly talented child, such a sacrifice may be justified.)

On the other hand, an activity we think is particularly worth after-school time is for an older child to take a part-time job related to a potential career. We're also sold on the benefits of volunteering in places like hospitals, senior citizen centers, and schools for the handicapped.

Teaching Your Child to Budget After-school Time

Here's a technique to improve children's use of time so there is some time left after work is done. A child takes a few minutes each day after school to complete a schedule as described below. Usually, before too long, he's managing his time better and can stop writing down his schedule.

While the schedule is easy to use, you should help your child get started. First, make up a form like the one below. You may want to make copies.

After-School Schedule

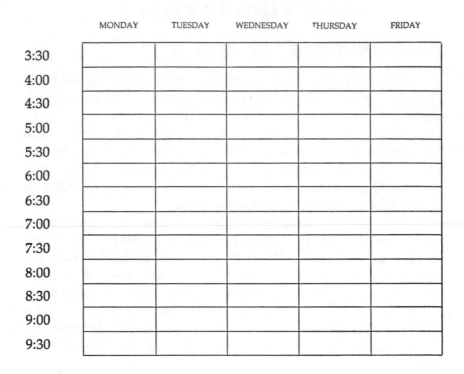

	MONDAY	TUESDAY	WEDNESDAY	THURSDAY	FRIDAY
3:30					
4:00					
4:30					
5:00					
5:30					
6:00					
6:30					
7:00					
7:30					
8:00					
8:30					
9:00					
9:30					

Then show your child how to complete it by walking him through the following directions:

1. On a piece of scratch paper, list each task you *must* do that day—each homework assignment, household responsibility, appointment, etc.

2. Estimate how long it will take to do each task. A rule of thumb is to add 25 percent to your best estimate, since there's only one way for a task to take as long as it should and an infinite number of ways for it to take longer. (A related principle: nothing takes five minutes.)

3. Insert each task into the schedule at a time that works best for you; for example, if you do your best thinking soon after school, that's when you should slot your hardest homework

assignment. Try to keep the study periods at the same times each day—ritual leads to habit.

4. Figure out how long you can usually concentrate without a break and then insert breaks appropriately, If you have trouble concentrating, start out with short work periods, even as short as five minutes. If you succeed at that, you can work a little longer the next time.

5. On the scratch paper, write down each thing you would *like* to do today.

6. Then rank each of these in importance. Put a "1" next to the think you'd most like to do, a "2" next to the thing you'd next like to do, etc.

7. Insert in your schedule as many of the things you'd like to do as will fit. But don't overschedule. Blanks in the schedule usually end up filled or if not, provide useful revitalization time.

Here's a sample completed schedule:

Stephanie's After-School Schedule: Monday

3:30 Snack and relax
4:00 Study for science test.
4:30 Work on Africa report.
5:00 Break until 5:15, then do math homework
5:30 Finish math homework, do spelling homework.
6:00 Set dinner table then free time.
6:30 Dinner
7:30 Watch "The Peoples Court"
8:00 Do reading homework. Gather all stuff for school.
8:30 Play with chemistry set or whatever.
9:00 Get ready for bed.
9:30 Lights out.

Note that as soon as Stephanie finished her homework, she gathered everything she needed to take to school the next day. If she's missing something, she may have time to get it. (She also puts it all in one assigned place so she can find it in the morning).

You don't want to hover over your child so he feels pressured in following his schedule. But it is a good idea at first, to check that he has a schedule and even to look it over to see that it is realistic. Also, about midway through his schedule, you might check to see how well he is meeting it. An occasional deviation is no cause for criticism.

If your child will use a written schedule for awhile, he should be able to figure out a timetable that will enable him to get his work done and still have time for fun.

Teaching Your Child to Get the Most Homework Done in the Least Time

Craig and Justine were equally good in math and equally disappointed when their teacher remembered to assign forty-four homework problems. But while Justine was working for over an hour, Craig worked so efficiently that he was out playing ball after thirty minutes.

What are the keys to efficiency? First, your child must want to be efficient, and he will if he realizes that inefficiency can cause him to spend twice as much time on homework as necessary. He also needs a workable system. If his system isn't working, you might review the following suggestions with him:

- Try setting up a written schedule as described above.

- To reduce temptation, your child should do homework cloistered in an "office," a quiet room. (A room isn't quiet if the television or radio is on, but we must admit to having done much homework with a rock 'n' roll accompaniment.) If your child needs quiet, and can't get it at home, a library or a friend's house may satisfy.

- His "office" should have a desk and a not too comfortable chair. (However, many successful students have been known to do homework sprawled on a bed or floor.)

- Good lighting comes cheap—ten to fifteen dollars for an architect's lamp. It clamps onto a desk and contorts freely so the light can fall in the right place.

- Before sitting down, your child should take care of:

a. hunger—a mind torn between food and homework usually chooses food;

b. fatigue—kids can sit sleepily for an hour over a twenty-minute assignment. Better to take a short nap first. Sometimes, just a five-minute break can get him back on track;

c. compelling preoccupation—your daughter may find it hard to concentrate on homework when she's just had a spat with her boyfriend; she may just have to talk it out first. Unfortunately, some kids develop "compelling" preoccupations on a daily basis, a marvelous tool for procrastination;

d. equipment—lots of time can be saved by a well-stocked desk. While doing her homework, Sarah's pen ran out of ink. There were none in her desk so she went to the kitchen to get one. There, she was reminded of the lemonade in the fridge—get the glass, get the ice cubes, get the lemonade, drink the lemonade—five minutes. On the way back, she saw her sister watching television and couldn't resist watching for "just a second"—ten minutes. Finally she got back to her desk, wondering what she had been doing before she stopped to get a pen.

Another key to getting homework done efficiently is knowing when, whom, and how to ask for help.

When: As soon as Richard reaches a problem where the answer doesn't immediately spew from his pen, he calls for help. In contrast, Susan never asks for help. The happy medium is clearly the solution. Much is learned from tackling something hard, but if after some extra effort, understanding still seems distant, it's time to get help.

Whom: Even if we're home, our daughter usually calls one of her study buddies—a network of the best students in her class. She knows that they often understand the assignment as well as we, and can be more patient, not to mention that they can be a pipeline to the latest gossip. Only as a last resort, does she ask us. If there's no one available to help, she skips that part of the homework and goes on.

How: To avoid cheating, our daughter asks a study buddy just for an explanation to get her on the right track. "Hi, Julie. I don't know how to do those ratio problems, numbers 16 through 20. Could you explain how to do one of them?" She also calls when she's not sure of the assignment. She would hate to do the wrong one.

The Parent's Role in Homework

Even if your child uses study buddies, you'll undoubtedly get some pleas for homework help. Here's how you might handle them.

It's very tempting for a child to give up and ask for a parent's help. But giving up quickly can become a lifelong habit. So, when you get the plea for help, first try to figure out if your child really needs it. Does the work look like something he could do by himself? Does his face, voice, and body language suggest a real need? Does he often ask for help even when he doesn't need it? If you think he can do it on his own, you might suggest a compromise by offering to check it after he finishes.

In most cases, it won't hurt your child to struggle solo through the homework, even if it means getting problems 2 through 6 wrong. The lessons he'll learn in self-reliance are probably more important than those he'd learn from getting problems 2 through 6 correct. Besides, he may even figure out how to do them himself.

When you decide to help, you can do it quickly and without tears by remembering that your job is merely to provide only enough help to enable your child to tackle the work on his own, even if it won't be perfect. Just give enough of a hint to get him on the right track.

Here are some other parent/homework hints:

- Don't sit with your child as he does his homework; that makes you too readily available as a homework assistant.

- When your child has asked you to explain something for the third time or when he gets mad at you for not explaining it clearly, it's easy to say things like, "Geez, I've explained it three times" or "Don't you understand it yet?" If you feel such words coming, it may be time to leave the room. But if you can muster a bit more patience, try to pinpoint the problem by asking *him* to explain how to do it, starting with the last thing he clearly understands. That way you can figure out the part he needs help on.

- After your child finishes his homework, you may want to check it occasionally, especially if it was a difficult assignment.

- If your child is having ongoing difficulty with homework, you might try a Three-Question Chat with your child about it. (See Chapter 2). Failing that, a note to the teacher may be in order. (See Chapter 3.)

Another useful approach to ongoing problems is to hire a tutor. Your child can probably get more individualized help in a one-hour tutoring session than in a month at school. But the tutor must be the right person, and professional credentials offer no guarantee. Yet, sometimes, a high school or college student, neighbor, church member, or even one of your child's friends can do a good job.

Before hiring, be sure the tutor is willing to confine the tutoring to the child's actual schoolwork. Some tutors want to use different materials, which means your child has to do his regular schoolwork plus the work the tutor piles on. The last thing your child wants is more work—if he needs a tutor, he's probably having enough difficulty just completing the regular work. Studies have shown that tutors just using the regular schoolwork can be very effective—unless the work is *much* too difficult.

For starters, try one session and sit in. Does the tutor explain things clearly? Your child doesn't need another teacher he can't understand. Is the tutor patient even when having to explain something for the third time? Does he seem to care whether your child learns or not?

Consider stopping the tutoring as soon as your child is over the major difficulty. Like all forms of assistance, tutoring can become addictive and make your child feel he can't make it on his own.

103

Showing Your Child How to Study For an A on Tests

Many people make fun of the "hyperconcerned" parent who worries because his fifth grader doesn't do well on classroom tests, but, as we saw with Greg earlier, doing poorly in the early grades can have long-range effects.

The following are study techniques that have been proven to increase test scores. They help all students learn more—even if they're already getting good grades—and can really help the weak student.

It's a shame that many children disregard these techniques. Educators have tried and tried to get kids to use them, with little success. But we hope you'll have more luck—perhaps concerned parents will have more influence than us teachers.

High on the list of important but little-followed techniques is the recommendation to start studying long before the test. Try to sell your child on the idea, but, even if you can't, all's not lost—if he knows how to study.

To avoid wasted study time, your child needs to know exactly what content will be covered on the test, whether the focus will be on memorization or understanding, and whether it will be short-answer or essay. Looking at previous tests made up by the same teacher can also be instructive. If your child isn't sure what to study, he should ask the teacher.

Second, your child can do some of his most effective studying with a study buddy, in person or on the phone. For you, this is good news and bad news: it may tie up your phone, but at least you will be free to pursue other activities besides memorizing the causes of the Civil War.

The following techniques apply only to specific kinds of tests. We'll divide tests into memorization tests, text/notes tests, and math tests.

Memorization Tests

All or part of many classroom tests are memorization tests. Spelling, vocabulary, grammar, and addition-fact tests are examples. A student has a big advantage if he memorizes well. Fortunately, the ability to memorize is not fixed. Almost all students can memorize better if they use the following study method:

Step 1: Find out what you already know

Many children waste time studying things they already know. Glen studied for a spelling test by writing each spelling word five times each, even though he knew fifteen of twenty beforehand. So, before studying for a memorization test, your child should get pretested to see how much of the material he needs to study. You or a study buddy can test him, but if he has a tape recorder, he can test himself:

He "makes up" the test by slowly reading into a tape recorder each item to be memorized followed by the answer; for example, "friend, f-r-i-e-n-d." After all items and answers have been recorded, he can test himself by listening to the item, turning off the tape recorder and trying to write the answer. He makes note of the items he gets wrong and proceeds to study only those items.

Step 2: How to study what you don't know

John and Ellen both needed to study five spelling words. John wrote each word ten times each while Ellen used a much more powerful method which nonetheless only took about a minute per word. Here's how Ellen studied the first word she had misspelled, "friend." She:

1. observed where her error was—she had spelled it "ei" instead of "ie,"
2. figured out a trick to help her remember—"fri end,"— "the end" of a "fry,"
3. said "f-r-I-E" aloud five times,
4. wrote the word five times,
5. closed her eyes and tried to picture it in her mind, and finally,
6. wrote it from memory and checked to be sure it was correct.

She then went on to repeat the process with the next word she had spelled incorrectly. After she had studied all five words, she tested herself using the tape recorder and restudied any words she got wrong.

Text/Notes Tests

Particularly in junior and senior high school, students take many text/notes tests, exams which focus on material covered in class lectures and/or in a textbook. These tests require more than memorization, so the previous technique won't suffice. Many students study by just reading their class notes and the text, but there's a better way:

Studying Class Notes

Even though it may be embarrassing to some, it's a good idea to read class notes aloud, repeating key phrases to help them sink in. Every page or so, your child should try to explain the material to a mirror, without referring to the notes. Most tests emphasize material covered in class, so time spent studying class notes is usually well spent.

Studying Text

Almost all educators agree that SQ3R is a most effective technique for studying text—it's a shame so few students use it. SQ3R can improve your child's grades all the way from late elementary school through graduate school. Here's a version to show your child. SQ3R stands for the five steps in studying text: survey, question, read, recite, and review.

1. Survey. Your child should first read each heading in the chapter to be studied and, if there is one, the summary at the beginning or end of the chapter. This only takes a minute, yet research indicates that this overview greatly facilitates understanding.

2. Question. Your child should reread the first heading in the chapter and turn it into a question: for example, "Learned and Unlearned Behavior" into "What behaviors don't we learn? Taking a few seconds to come up with this question provides a focus for reading and can arouse curiosity.

3. Read. The next step is to read the material under the heading. Everyone does this part, but some things can make the reading more productive:

- Your child should read primarily to answer the question derived from the heading.

106

- He should skim easy or unimportant passages, silently read the bulk, and read aloud (whispering is all right) important or difficult passages.

- Most speed reading courses spend considerable time teaching students to read groups of words, rather than one word at a time. Your child might consciously work on this.

- Most students know the importance of studying words in italics or boldface. But few students carefully look at tables, graphs, and pictures. These are often the keys to understanding—sometimes a picture is indeed worth a thousand words.

- Your child should frequently ask himself, "Am I understanding what I'm reading?" or "Do I remember what I just read?" and reread if he finds himself blank.

- It's a good idea to take notes using phrases, not complete sentences. A rule of thumb is to write only a few lines for each average page of text.

- He should not take notes on material he already knows. Doing so means unnecessary work taking the note and rereading the note.

- Writing should be legible or he won't want, or be able to, read his notes when it's time to review.

- If your child owns the book, a yellow highlight marker offers a simple way to take notes on text. He should only mark key phrases, perhaps 10 to 20 percent per average page of text. If more than one line is important, he needn't highlight it all but can just put a bracket next to the lines.

- If it is the school's book, with the teacher's permission he might put a dot in pencil next to each important line on a page, erasing them before returning the book.

4. Recite. After reading the material under each heading, your child should answer *aloud* the question he made up from the heading, using as many main ideas, supporting details, and important vocabulary as possible. This is the hardest but most important step, and the one the fewest students do. Reciting is the best way for your child to know if he really understands the material. If he can't recite the material adequately, he has instant feedback that he needs to reread it.

5. Review. Finally your child should reread his notes or highlighted material (not the entire text) to cement the key content in memory.

After repeating the SQ3R process for each heading's worth of text, your child might call his study buddy and take turns asking each other potential test questions. Students have told us that this is helpful and fun. It's also the acid test—students' questions tend to be harder than any the teachers would ask.

Math Tests

Terry studied for a math test by doing twenty problems—all incorrectly. Roger's studying for the same test was no more useful—he had completely forgotten how to divide fractions. He spent all his study time trying in vain to decipher his notes and textbook. There's a better way:

First, on his own, your child should memorize any formulas or other information he'll need for the test. Then, he and his study buddy should get together, independently do a problem from the text or worksheets, and then check to see if their answers match; matching answers are usually correct. If the answers are different, they should review the problem together, step-by-step. After getting a few items of one type correct, they can move on to another type likely to show up on the test. If there's a need for additional practice problems, they can make up their own—sometimes it's as simple as adding "1" to each number in a problem in the text.

It may be a challenge to get your child to use these techniques for successful studying, but the payoffs for high test scores are great. Higher test scores lead to better class placements, and the success cycle is placed in motion. But don't try to change all your child's study habits overnight. Start with the subject he's having the most difficulty with and let him see for himself the rewards that good study techniques can bring.

Painless Papers

"I'm assigning the following report . . ." These words have filled countless students with painful visions of frustrating hours in the library, amassing and organizing facts of little interest. "No groaning, now; it can't hurt that much. Writing a paper not only helps you learn the material you're writing about, but teaches you how to do research, organize it, and present it clearly in writing. Besides, your report card grade largely depends on it."

This pep talk rarely reduces the pain. Children often react by repressing thought of the paper until just before the due date when they race to the encyclopedia and crank out the required number of pages, padding with pictures, construction paper, and a fancy cover.

Scholars write papers for a living and so must use an efficient system for writing good ones. Their standard plan divides the huge task into ten little ones.[1] A child is also more likely to write a good paper and get it in on time if he sees it as a series of small manageable assignments, "Today I just have to _____."

Our daughter has used this method successfully to write papers in elementary and junior high school. We used a variation in graduate school and in writing this book.

Step 1: Get the assignment

Even if it's a shorty, misunderstanding the assignment hurts. But the pain is excruciating if the assignment is a research paper. Your child can avoid this by making sure he knows exactly what's required in the paper: the range of allowable topics, information required, format, and length.

Step 2: Define the topic

Your child should try to select a topic that, while still within the assigned limits, is something he's interested in. If he's interested in the topic, writing the paper will be less odious.

Another way to reduce paper pain is to choose a topic of appropriate breadth. "The Civil War" is too broad to be covered

---

[1] This is an adaptation of the procedure described in, Colligan, L. *The A+ Guide to Research and Term Papers.* N.Y.: Scholastic Book Service, ©1981.

adequately in the standard five- to ten-page paper, while "Civil War Uniforms" can probably be exhausted in a page. At a secondary school level, "The Causes of The Civil War" may be about right. An encyclopedia can often help your child select a topic of interest and of appropriate breadth.

Step 3: Write a thesis statement

It's rather painful to write (or read) a paper that is just a series of facts strung together. A paper should always express a point of view. To develop one, your child may need to do some reading, perhaps in an encyclopedia or other general reference. Then he should write a one-sentence statement, possibly a controversial one, of his point of view; for example, "The Civil War was more than a fight over slavery."

Step 4: Select subtopics

Dividing the paper into subtopics makes the task of researching a paper easier and also provides a structure for the reader. The writer should choose the subtopics that will support his thesis and be appropriately broad. For the thesis "The Civil War was more than a fight over slavery," subtopics might be: agricultural causes, manufacturing causes, political causes.

Step 5: Research each subtopic:

a. Find enough books or articles for each subtopic. Good sources are the card catalog, *the Reader's Guide to Periodical Literature*, the *New York Times Index*, and most importantly, the research librarian.

b. Scan each book or article's table of contents, index, or boldface headings to find the parts with information on the subtopic. Read only those parts that promise relevant and interesting information.

c. In phrase form, write each piece of information along with the author's name and page number on a separate index card. Also write a card for each idea the reading triggers. The cards can later be rearranged in a logical order for presentation in the paper. If a bibliography is required, an additional card should be written for each reference used, using standard form. (See the samples on page 111.) When your child has written sufficient note cards for all his subtopics, he can leave the library without the pain of lugging heavy volumes home.

Sample Note Card

CATTON, p. 53

AGRICULTURAL CAUSES

North & West states favored free farms for new settlers. South was against.

Sample Bibliography Card for a Book

Catton, B. The Centennial History of the Civil War.

3 vols. N.Y. : Doubleday, 1961-65.

Sample Bibliography Card for a Periodical

Peck, I. Divisions in a Divided House. Senior

Scholastic. v. 114, 3-5+, Feb. 5, 1982.

Step 6 (optional): Interview an expert

A paper comes alive when it presents information obtained from a person. Besides, doing an interview is fun. So, after your child has read about his topic, he might want to interview an expert—in our Civil War example, possibly a college professor or member of a local historical society. The key to a successful interview is preparing good questions in advance. Qualified subjective comments in particular can enrich a paper. He should take notes, one idea per note card.

Step 7: Organize the note cards

Your child should sort his note cards by subtopic and then arrange each subtopic's note cards in a logical order. If a card doesn't seem to fit anywhere, it should be put aside for possible use later. Not all ideas come from research, so at this stage, he may think of other ideas to include in the paper, putting each on an index card and inserting it in the proper place.

Most treatises on writing papers stress the importance of an outline. Indeed, schools spend considerable time teaching students how to outline. Yet in our experience, we've found that by choosing subtopics as we've recommended in step 3 and in organizing one's note cards as we've suggested here, the outline becomes unnecessary, at least for papers below college level.

Step 8: Write a rough draft

(Your child may find this step's information useful in all writing, not just research papers.) First, your child should try to choose a title. Choosing a title at this point will focus his writing and is a painless way to get started. A title should summarize the content, be playful, get the reader's attention, or, ideally, all three. A possible title for our report on the causes of the Civil War might be, "The Civil War: Not a Black and White Issue."

Sometimes, it's easier to write the introduction after the paper is written, but usually it's done first. The first sentence should be a grabber; for example, a startling fact, authoritative quote, interesting anecdote, or provocative question. Then, the introduction should present the thesis statement, briefly explain why the topic is important, and how the information will be presented; that is, list the subtopics.

The body of the paper is simply a translation of the note cards into smooth paragraphs. Phrases and sentences should be added to connect logically the information from the note cards. Additional ideas that come to mind can also be incorporated as long as they're inserted in a logical place. Each subtopic should be marked with a heading and if the subtopics are long, additional subheadings should be used.

A rule of thumb is to use many interesting verbs and few adjectives, especially adjectives that communicate little: "boring," "good," "nice," "fantastic." "The anecdote made me feel like Madame Curie when she discovered radium," is more communicative than, "The anecdote was fantastic."

The paper should end with a brief conclusion that reviews the major points leading to the thesis. The last sentence should leave the reader feeling satisfied, that he's completed something of value.

Step 9: Edit the rough draft

The next thing to do is wait. One or two days' distance from the paper can restore a sense of objectivity and, perhaps, even renewed interest. Then, your child should carefully reread the rough draft *aloud* twice, one time for content, one time for grammar and mechanics, each time penciling in all changes.

Often, a writer suspects he's being unclear but doesn't know how to clarify. Here are a few suggestions:

- Lack of clarity is often the result of unnecessary words; the good writer looks to eliminate every one.

- In unclear sections, add summaries or boldface headings, shorten overly long sentences and paragraphs.

- The connection between seemingly unrelated sentences or paragraphs can be made clearer by adding connectives such as: because, although, but, therefore, for example, and, in other words.

Step 10: Write the final draft

Teachers are usually reluctant to give a low grade to a paper that appears carefully done. An easy way to make a paper appear that way is to write very neatly (typing is better, word processing is best) a final draft of the paper and enclose it in an attractive cover.

Ten steps sound like a lot. But this method ends up faster and produces better grades than the more haphazard approaches often taken. It promises maximum gain for minimum pain.

Nothing can take the place of the Cleavers, but we feel better knowing that we've taught our daughter these proven techniques for getting homework done fast and well. She is usually able to get her work done by early evening so we can go out for ice cream, watch "St. Elsewhere," or dance around the house to '50s music. A three-way Lindy is much more fun than struggling with problem 47.

PART III:

Choose Your Child's Public School and Teacher

It seems as though you can't go to a party without the conversation coming around to about what's wrong with the public schools. We're always hearing about some parent's struggles to make sure his child is in the right schools or avoids the wrong teacher—parents know that schools and teachers are the keys to a good education.

One parent told us about his painful hours fighting the principal and school district to get his child out of a bad teacher's class; he even threatened to pull his child out of public school and to file a lawsuit, all to no avail.

A second parent told us about how she got her child into a desired public school by renting a nearby garage so she could show an address in that school's attendance area.

A third parent battled with the principal to get her child into a desired teacher's class and won, so she thought; her daughter ended up hating the teacher.

A fourth parent would have liked her child to attend a particular public school but was told it was full, so she just gave up and is now spending $6,000 a year on private school and wonders if it's worth it.

Many parents just take potluck and accept whatever the public schools give them even though they know their children's education is inadequate.

There's no need to make Hobson's choice. This part of the book will show you how to tell if your child's school and teachers are giving him the education he deserves and, if not, how to get him better schools and teachers, legally and without having to battle the schools. We believe that ensuring that our daughter was in the right public school with the right teachers was among the most valuable things we've ever done for our child.

CHAPTER EIGHT

Choose Your Child's Teacher

Your child's teacher can make a big difference. In fourth grade, Heather complained about school nearly every day; in fifth grade, her most frequent school comment was, "Mom, look at my work!" In first grade, Angela frequently had a stomachache on school mornings; in second grade, she had none. In tenth grade, Wendy talked about going to Harvard; in the eleventh grade, she wanted to go to community college and "be a nothing." In second grade, Eric's teacher said that he was hyperactive and should be considered for special education; in third grade, his teacher said he was doing beautifully and was a pleasure to have in the class.

Unfortunately, there are many poor teachers firmly ensconced in the schools, particularly in the public schools. For instance, one-third of credentialed teachers in California fail the ninth-grade-level basic skills test. Making matters worse, incompetent teachers are virtually impossible to fire—only eighty-six public school teachers were fired for incompetence from 1939 to 1982 across all fifty states!

But, statistics may not bring to life how powerful an effect incompetent teachers can have on children. Consider this story told to us by a parent who is also a teacher.

Ethan had good experiences in the first through third grades, which made me pretty confident that I didn't need to choose his teachers, even after I heard mixed reviews about his fourth-grade teacher; let's call her Mrs. Malapede. I basically ignored Ethan's fourth-grade complaints until they got just too frequent and too intense, whereupon I decided to visit Mrs. Malapede's class.

My memory of that visit remains painfully clear. The bell rang at 8:30. 8:31, 8:32. Why wasn't she starting? 8:33. Finally, Mrs. Malapede's first words, in a chalk-squeak voice, blaming the children unfairly: "Quiet yourselves, young people! Don't you know the bell has rang? [sic] Peggy Phillips?" "Here." "Linda Cederborg?" "Here." "Ethan Jordan?" "Present." Twenty seven names and five minutes later, she finished. Her voice was bad enough; I could imagine listening to that for 180 school days, but, in addition, she spoke so slowly. It almost seemed as though she was trying to waste class time.

"All right, young people. Monday is Columbus Day, so today we're going to learn some about Columbus." [sic— she doesn't even chalk-squeak in good English!] I'm going to read aloud from this book about Christopher Columbus. [She reads.]

'Christopher Columbus was born sometime between August 25th and October 31st, 1451 in Genoa, then the capital of an independent Italian republic. The family name was Colombo. In English, he is known by the Latin form of his name, Columbus. He called himself, Cristóbal Colón after he settled in Spain. His father, Domenico Colombo, was a wool weaver who took a leading part in the affairs of his local guild. His mother, Susanna Fontanarossa, was the daughter of a wool weaver . . .'

She droned on, Gregorian chant-like, for fifteen interminable minutes. There had to be more important things to learn about Columbus and more interesting ways to teach them.

Then Mrs. Malapede handed out two worksheets, slowly, of course. "All right, young people, let's look at the first one." "Which one is the first one?" asked one child. A reasonable question. "No calling out," she sighed. "This one!" She "explained" how to do the worksheets although I wouldn't have been able to do them, before or after her "explanations."

118

"Any questions?" Predictably, lots of hands shot up. "If you had listened the first time, you wouldn't have to ask questions!" Before the wave of hands would subside, she had to explain the directions twice more. More time wasted. If she couldn't make the directions clearer, she shouldn't have used those worksheets. Besides, they were teaching trivia. I suspect the main thing the entire lesson taught was that learning about Columbus was boring.

The class began working and Mrs. Malapede continued to answer questions. "Is this right?" "No, Johnny. Next time you'll listen more carefully. Now figure it out by yourself." I was surprised that he'd try it again after such help, but he did and his next try was a big improvement. But Mrs. Malapede only focused on the negative, "No, it's still wrong. Do it again." It almost seemed as if Mrs. Malapede wanted him to fail and certainly wasn't helping him succeed.

Some who still didn't understand the cryptic directions, chatted while waiting for Mrs. Malapede. A few others fomented minor turmoil, having decided not to do the worksheet at all. Maybe they figured that Mrs. Malapede was too harried to do much about it or even to find out. The most aggressive ones did things like slam their pencils down, proclaiming, "This is boring!" or asked, "Do we have to do this?" More passive-aggressive types politely asked, "Can I use the bathroom?" or "How much time 'til lunch?" One child took an extended trip to the pencil sharpener, a trip which resembled a candidate working the crowd: strolling down the aisle, smiling, reaching out to touch as many someones as possible. Finally, he sharpened his pencils, a fistful, in slow motion.

A few of the early finishers had their hands up to inform Mrs. Malapede that they were done. The more sophisticated ones however, kept that fact to themselves and joined the rabble-rousers, knowing their reward for finishing early would just be another assignment for extra credit.

With each passing moment, the number of nonworkers and decibels increased despite Mrs. Malapede's frantic attempts to criticize and scare the class into compliance. "How will you ever get to be somebody? Get to work or else!" "Or else, what, Mrs. Malapede?"

It was chaos bordering on a zoo. I thought the lesson was finally over when Mrs. Malapede said, "Turn in your papers. I'll correct and return them in a few days." But then a child yelled, "Wait! I need two more minutes." "All right, finish up." So twenty-nine kids had to waste more time waiting for one to finish.

At 9:10 I left. It had only been forty minutes and, to think, those kids had five more hours of this. That day. And 180 more days like it! I felt pretty guilty that I hadn't visited the fourth grade teachers the previous spring. I'm not sure I could have chosen Ethan's teacher, but I'll bet I could have kept him from getting Mrs. Malapede."

Of course, most teachers are far better than Mrs. Malapede, but there are some pretty bad ones out there, even in good schools. Your child will probably survive a year with a Mrs. Malapede, especially if he is bright and well motivated. He may simply be bored and a bit unhappy, and in October he may start counting the days left in the school year. Of course, these reasons alone are worth the short time it takes to get your child a good teacher.

But, for many children, a year with a Mrs. Malapede can have more serious and enduring effects. He might not learn important skills or prerequisites for other skills. For example, if he doesn't learn his multiplication tables in the third grade, he won't be able to do division in the fourth.

Your child's too frequently hearing, "You *still* can't do that?" and "Can't you sit in your seat?" can affect his self-esteem. A Mrs. Malapede can open a child's eyes to the possibility of doing little work or even defying the teacher without serious consequence. She can cause a child to lose respect for the schools—the teacher, once seen as gold, can be understood as gold plated. She might even be the last straw that turns a child off to school for good.

Mrs. Malapede is an extreme example, but the effects of a good versus a poor teacher are great enough to warrant taking a little time each year to avoid the Mrs. Malapedes, if only as a kindness to your child.

Many people take the time to read reviews to ensure a few worthwhile hours at a movie, at a play, or with a book. Shouldn't you review a teacher to ensure that your child's next 180 school days are worthwhile?

Should You Try to Choose Every Teacher?

Most principals won't allow you to choose your child's teacher every year, so you probably needn't bother trying. Even if you ask in just the right way, you can typically convince a principal only every few years. Fortunately, most years you don't need to handpick. There may be little difference among the possible teachers or there may be no choice at all; for example, there may only be one teacher of a fifth-grade class with students on your child's level.

But, how do you decide which years you're going to try to choose? If your child is complaining bitterly about the current year's teacher, you may want to observe the teacher to help decide if a transfer is warranted.

Absent such urgencies, you should only select a teacher for the next school year. Consider choosing when you've heard horror stories about a Mrs. Malapede, or glowing reports about a Mrs. Magnapede who teaches the grade your child is about to enter.

If your child's school has Open School Days, it's worth observing next year's possible teachers to find out for yourself if they differ enough to justify trying to get your child into a particular class.

In this chapter, you'll learn how to decide if a teacher is right for your child after just one visit to the classroom. You'll also find out how to get the principal to place him in the class of your choice.

How Some Parents Judge Teachers

Many parents believe they know who the good teachers are at their child's school, but they're often mistaken. Some such parents rely on reputation, but teachers can build a good reputation because of factors that have little to do with their teaching ability; for example, toughness, a pleasant demeanor, or frequently sending newsletters home that advertise classroom highlights. And it could be that another parent will correctly rave about a teacher, yet that same teacher may be a poor choice for *your* child. Perhaps her child thrives with a laissez-faire teacher while your child requires a firmer hand.

Our sixty-nine-year-old neighbor described his eighth-grade English teacher, a teacher with a bad reputation. She never smiled and probably didn't like children; no foolishness was brooked in her class. Her appearance matched her severe manner: she was tall and spare, her Roman nose and cold eyes always seeming to bore in on you. Her hair was always pulled back in perfect austerity, an image completed by her stiff gray or black clothes.

She wanted everyone to believe she was an aristocrat. Though it was said that she had never been east of Boston, she had a hint of a lord's British accent. She didn't walk, she strode with studied grace, up and down the aisles with her questions.

Always those questions. The kids were always a little scared of her, but when she got to your aisle, and when she called on you, you felt the way an adult feels the first time he has to speak in public. Almost nobody liked her. One could certainly say she had a bad reputation.

But my neighbor believes she was the best teacher he ever had. Now, with fifty years' hindsight, he concludes that, "She taught me that literature was something to be sought for its own sake; it was something good. She gave me an appreciation of the beauty and precision of language when used properly and not sloppily. She gave me an outlook I hadn't had before that was a glimpse into the world of refinement and grace. No, not the snobbery, just an alternative to the ways of the working class fellows I grew up with."

Reputation is something to consider but not to rely on. To avoid relying purely on reputation, other parents observe teachers in action but also base their judgement on poor indices of teacher quality. They might, for example, be swayed by an attractive classroom when, in fact, children can receive an excellent education in a classroom with that lived-in look and without snazzy bulletin boards.

Some parents are also erroneously turned off by a class that isn't church quiet. It suggests to them that the class is out of control. Noise can signify a class out of control. But it can also signify important learning. Some things can best be learned noisily; for example, when a group is working together to construct a model city. So the question is not whether the class is noisy but why?

Finally, we all know we shouldn't judge a book by its cover, yet it's easy to be affected by people's outward appearance. Many parents judge teachers by their covers: their ravaged complexions, brusque veneer, an unneeded twenty pounds, or clothes by K-Mart rather than Claiborne. Judging by these factors, few parents would want their child to have my neighbor's eighth-grade English teacher.

How should you judge? Shortly, we'll suggest relevant criteria in what we call the Teacher Report Card, but first, something should be said about timing.

When to Observe

If you're contemplating choosing next year's teacher for your child, there are three prime times for observation, each with advantages and disadvantages. The easiest time is during Open School Days or whenever the public is invited to view classes in session. No appointment is necessary and you know you are welcome.

Some parents are concerned that observing a teacher, especially during an Open School Day, is not representative of his typical performance because he'll put on a show for the visiting adults. This is less true than one might expect. While teachers may try harder, the extra effort can't turn a poor teacher into an excellent one. When we visited our daughter's fourth-grade class during Open School Week, the class spent half an hour tracing a map from a textbook while the teacher hung bulletin boards. If this was the teacher trying to impress us, imagine her on an off day! When I supervised student teachers, I saw the full range of teaching quality, even though the student teachers knew they were being judged and that their credentials hung in the balance. Somehow, you either have the skill or you don't. They may try to impress you with a little fancier lesson plan or an extra, "Good, Johnny," but you can still tell approximately how good the teacher is. When your child is ice skating and sees that you're watching her, she may try harder, but you still can tell she's not Debi Thomas.

A more significant disadvantage of observing during Open School Days is that you're not sure whom to observe—will Mrs. Magnapede still be teaching fourth grade next year? Your best bet is to observe the teachers who currently teach the grade your child will be entering, and hope Mrs. Ginsburg doesn't get pregnant and Mr. Chan doesn't decide he's tired of teaching sixth grade.

A better alternative is to observe teachers a few weeks before the end of the school year, when next year's teaching assignments are coming clear. If, after your observations, you decide to request a teacher, make your request during the week before school starts. At that time, teaching assignments will be firm, but it's easy for the principal to move your child to another class.

In days of yore, it was rare to see a parent visiting a classroom except during Open School Days, but in many of today's schools, it is routine. In such schools, a quick call to the school secretary may set up your visit. If you need to give a reason for visiting, as always in dealing with school people, tact is the key. Here's how one parent worded her request:

"This hasn't been the best of school years for my child, and I could use a bit of reassurance about next year. It would really help if I could spend a few minutes in Mrs. Magnapede's and Mrs. Malapede's class."

If for whatever reason, the principal doesn't allow you to visit classes (don't accept a "no" from the secretary), you might ask the secretary for the names and phone numbers of parents who are active in each classroom of interest. Get their rating of the teacher by asking them the eight yes/no questions on the Teacher Report Card.

How to Rate a Teacher: The Teacher Report Card

Now we'll suggest what to look for as you observe the teacher in action: eight crucial characteristics in the good teacher, which, when taken together, are the Teacher Report Card. Knowing what to look for enables you to learn more in one brief visit than from hours of unfocused observation, and to learn enough to decide reasonably if a teacher is right for your child. You needn't memorize what to look for; the eight items are listed in abbreviated form on a tiny "shopping list" which you can take on your classroom visit.

While the Teacher Report Card could validly be used to rate all teachers, it's probably most practical in the elementary grades, when a child typically has only one main teacher. In junior and senior high school, your child usually has many teachers, so we've developed an even simpler method for selecting secondary school teachers, which is presented later in this chapter.

Your Visit

You want to see the teacher in action, not while he's showing a film, giving a test, monitoring silent reading time, etc. You can increase your chances by visiting during the first two hours of the morning. If you're planning to visit more than one classroom, before entering one, peek in or listen to see if this is a good time. If not, try another class first. If this is the only class you're visiting, just go in and wait until the teacher resumes active teaching; most classroom activities don't last very long.

Once in the classroom, identify one or two children who seem similar to your child in ability and/or disposition and interpret each Teacher Report Card item particularly as it applies to them. For example, "Are the children, especially those like mine, working hard yet contentedly?" Identifying the reaction of children like your own is important because, for example, a teacher may be fine with bright children but poor with slow or unmotivated ones—you want to find a teacher that is right for *your* child.

The Teacher Report Card

The eight yes/no questions on the Teacher Report Card are presented with an explanation of why each is important and how you can answer them in your brief visit. Don't be concerned if, after your visit, you can't answer every question. You'll still have learned enough to make a more valid choice than if you judged the teacher merely on reputation or on an unfocused observation.

The following information has a second use. It is essentially a short course on what constitutes good teaching which can make you a more knowledgeable member of a school or school district committee.

Question 1: Are students spending most of their time on worthwhile activities?

Studies have shown that the average percentage of class time spent on learning tasks is as high as 85 percent with some teachers and as low as 20 percent with others. High percentages result from a number of factors that you might look for in your classroom visits:

- Maintaining good discipline. Some teachers need to use only an occasional glare to maintain order while others need to spend half the period begging students to pay attention.

- Spending the minimum time on noninstructional matters. Some teachers take attendance by quickly noting which seats are empty. Others take ten times as long, calling out thirty students' names.

- Beginning instruction as soon as the bell rings and continuing until the very end of the period. Some teachers cherish every minute, teaching until the bell rings, while other teachers allow students to pack up a few minutes before the end of the period.

- Quick transitions between activities. In some classes, only a few seconds separate the end of one lesson from the beginning of another. In other classes, a change of activity means five minutes of dead time.

- Students knowing what they're supposed to do. After a teacher gives instructions, are many students raising their hands or whispering to each other because they still don't know what to do? When students finish their work early, do they sit around chatting, or do they go on to another assignment?

Some classrooms have high on-task rates, but too many of the tasks aren't worthwhile. It's not a good sign if the class you observe is learning that on June 18, 1812, the U.S. declared war on Great Britain, on October 13, 1812, British forces won the Battle of Queenston Heights, and on April 27, 1813, the Americans captured York.

In contrast, be encouraged if you notice an emphasis on broad concepts and thinking skills. A good indication is a teacher who frequently asks questions that go beyond the factual—"When should the Americans have invaded?" "Why did the turtle feel he needed to make that promise?" "What could we do to improve this scene in our play?"

Question 2: Are students working hard yet contentedly?

We'd all like our children to develop an interest in learning, to develop a work ethic, and to be reasonably happy in school. You can tell how successful a teacher is in fostering all three by simply observing whether the students appear to be working hard yet contentedly. Are most kids sitting up straight and alert, involved in their work, eager to participate in class discussions, willing to stop for a momentary laugh, but not one lasting five minutes? Or are they slouching, sighing, looking up at the clock, and slowly pushing their pencils like a disgruntled employee two days from retirement?

Question 3: Does the teacher appear to care about the children?

Even though a student's success or failure may sometimes be beyond a teacher's control, good teachers believe they can make a difference. This belief generally makes them more caring, enthusiastic, and committed to their jobs; they work harder in preparing lessons, grading work, and teaching itself.

You can get clues to how caring a teacher is by asking yourself, "Does it look like the teacher put much effort into creating or teaching the lesson? Are the bulletin boards attractive and do they show off interesting student assignments, or are they just covered to be covered—for example, with a series of travel posters? Does the teacher seem genuinely pleased when a student does even a little thing well, and disappointed and helpful when he doesn't quite make it?"

An example of the latter occurred when a student was called to the front of the class to describe the contents of a jar with silkworm cocoons inside. The jar slipped from his hands and smashed into bits. He stood there in shock, bracing for the teacher's response. She said, "You must feel terrible, I know. Not long ago, I dropped a jar of mayonnaise in the supermarket. You haven't seen a mess until you've seen a quart of mayonnaise all over the floor. Everyone saw me and the mess. I was so embarrassed."

Unfortunately, there are other teachers who believe they can't make much difference in their students. These teachers are quick to explain away a student's or even an entire class's poor performance as beyond the teacher's control. We've heard a million excuses in the teacher's room: "They come from terrible homes." "It's raining." "It's spring." "It's a full moon." "It's just after the weekend." "It's just before the weekend." "It's the midweek blues."

These teachers are less likely to work hard. When a child is having difficulty, they give up easily and let the child know in subtle and not so subtle ways that he's hopeless. We have actually heard a teacher say each of the following to a child in front of the entire class: "Come on! You're in the sixth grade. A third grader could do that problem." "You'll always be an idiot if you keep that up!" "No, not you, Johnny. I need someone I can count on."

Your child's self-esteem and attitude toward school can nosedive if he's a frequent target of a teacher's scorn. Even if your child is never the target, such a teacher is hardly a good role model for your child.

Question 4: Does the teacher address individual student needs?

Here are some clues to look for:

- Asking the class questions of varying difficulty. If a third grade teacher was teaching a lesson on action verbs, he might alternate between low-level questions like, "Who can give me an example of an action verb?" and higher-level questions like, "When would you want to use 'giggle' instead of 'laugh'?"

- Teaching by showing as well as telling helps the visual and the auditory learner.

- Dividing the class into two or three groups of different ability. (Dividing them into more than three groups brings about serious problems, as will be discussed in Chapter 9.)

- Varying the difficulty of assignments for more and less able students. Bright students should get the same amount of work as other kids, but on a higher level. It's not fair to reward the first kids in the class to memorize the names of the presidents with the privilege of memorizing vice-presidents. If a teacher gives everyone the same assignment, there should at least be challenging extra-credit work for early finishers, not just more work on the same level.

Question 5: Is the teacher well educated in the subject he teaches and in general?

Too many teachers aren't sufficiently knowledgeable in their fields. Some don't even have adequate basic skills. The extent of the problem is suggested by results of the CBEST, the basic skills test all teachers in California are required to pass prior to certification. Here is an item from the CBEST:

There are fourteen boys and twelve girls in Mr. Gomez's sixth grade class. With only this information, which of the following problems about Mr. Gomez's class CANNOT be solved?

(A) What is the average age of the students?
(B) How many students are there in the class?
(C) How many more boys than girls are there?
(D) What percent of the students are boys?
(E) What is the ratio of number of girls to number of boys?

One-third of already credentialed teachers who take the CBEST fail, so we can't assume that all teachers possess basic skills, let alone competence in their subject area. So in your visit, you might look for signs of how educated the teacher is. Does he use correct standard English? Are there misspelled words on the chalkboard? Does he constantly refer to notes when lecturing? How well does he answer student questions? Does he appear to be a bright, interesting person with whom your child would find it profitable to spend 180 school days?

Question 6: Would this teacher's level of firmness be good for my child?

Some adults need someone standing over them, telling them exactly what to do and making sure they're doing it. Others can receive an assignment and be self-propelled for days. Children are no different. An anxious or well-motivated child may be best off with a teacher that applies little external pressure, while a less motivated child might react to such a teacher by doing little work.

While firmness doesn't always manifest itself in the same way, here is a portrait of one very firm teacher to give you an idea of how, in your brief classroom visit, you might distinguish a firm teacher from a permissive teacher:

Mr. Boxer wants to retain direct control of what everyone is doing, so there is little independent seatwork in his class. Most of the time, he teaches lessons to the entire class, seemingly aware of exactly what everyone in the class is doing at any moment. In Mr. Boxer's class, students must sit straight and tall, speak loud and clear. The rules are clear, enforced, and rarely bent. He frequently asks questions and calls on not only the few kids who always raise their hands, but also the quiet ones in the back, to make sure they're staying with him. He accepts no half-hearted answers and pushes each child to the extent of his ability. Mr. Boxer's standards extend to nearly every phase of the classroom. He grades almost all work and keeps accurate records. Accountability is the watchword in his class—everything counts toward the report card. Everyone knows Mr. Boxer is the captain and that he runs a tight ship.

Mr. Boxer could be the best teacher for an undisciplined child and the worst one for a nervous, creative child.

Question 7: Is the teacher's gender beneficial to my child?

Just as some students are better off with a firmer or more permissive teacher, some are better off with a male or female. For example, in many single-parent households, children lack a positive male role model. A good male teacher might be just the ticket.

Question 8: Do students give the teacher high marks?

It's worth getting the student viewpoint, especially after the first few grades. After all, they are the consumers of the teacher's services and have seen him in action for many days.

You probably have heard the student consensus from your child or from other parents. But if not, you can get it by calling one or two parents of students in the class. If you don't already know some parents with children in that teacher's class, you can get a phone number or two from the PTA directory or even from the school secretary.

Phone calls to parents have yielded such interesting reactions as these: "All the children love Miss Jones. She works them very hard but somehow they don't seem to mind." "Most of the children like her but my child doesn't. He says that she only pays attention to the dumb kids." "Kathy loves the teacher but the main reason seems to be that the class plays around most of the time."

While on the phone with a parent, you might ask for his general impressions, or ask him some questions from the Teacher Report Card. Some additional questions of interest that you can't answer from your classroom observation are, "Is most schoolwork corrected?" "Does the teacher provide many comments on written work?" "Does he require students to correct their work?"

Question 9: Are there other factors that should be considered in reviewing the teacher?

You may have special concerns. Here are some examples:

- Your child loves science and the teacher specializes in it.

- Your child has been doing poorly in reading despite tons of phonics, so you want him to have a teacher who uses non-phonetic approaches to teach reading.

- Your child would like to have this teacher.

- You and the teacher are friends.

Now for the Teacher Report Card. You can probably make a valid choice just using the questions as guidelines, but a numerical grading system is provided for those who prefer it. An abbreviated list of the questions—the "shopping list"—is provided for you to take on your classroom visits.

The Teacher Report Card: Shopping List
1. Working hard yet contentedly
2. Time spent on worthwhile learning
3. Teacher caring
4. Teacher addresses individual needs
5. Teacher well educated
6. Level of firmness
7. Teacher gender
8. Student rating
9. Other factor(s)

Teacher Report Card

_____   _____
Teacher's name   Date

Directions: Simply use the questions to focus your classroom visit, or circle the appropriate score for each question.

	Yes	Partially or Not Sure	No
1. Are the children working hard yet contentedly?	15	8	0
2. Are most children engaged in worthwhile learning most of the time?	20	10	0
3. Does the teacher care about the children?	10	5	0
4. Does the teacher address students' individual needs?	10	5	0
5. Is the teacher well educated in the subject he's teaching and in general?	10	5	0
6. Would this teacher's level of firmness be good for my child?	10	5	0
7. Is this teacher's gender good for my child?	10	5	0
8. Do the students give the teacher high marks?	15	8	0

9. Is there another factor(s) that should be considered in rating this teacher? (If you're scoring, add or subtract an appropriate number of points)

_____   _____
Factor   Points

If you're scoring and would like to assign a letter grade to the teacher, add up the points for all the questions and compare the total score with the following charts:

Total Score	Letter Grade	Total Score	Letter Grade	Total Score	Letter Grade
90+	A	68-79	C	under 60	F
80-89	B	60-68	D		

Choosing Teachers in Junior and Senior High School

The stakes are lower in junior and senior high school since your child probably has each teacher for less than an hour a day. As long as your child is in the appropriate level of classes, it's less important to handpick your child's secondary school teachers.

We've found that you can avoid the very worst and get the very best, quickly and with reasonable accuracy, by simply asking your child's counselor or other person who programs your child into classes, "Are there any teachers you think would be particularly appropriate or inappropriate for my child?" You might also poll other parents, your child, or his friends. By the time kids reach junior high school age, they often know the really good and really bad teachers.

If you've found a teacher you're sure would be significantly better for your child, tactfully ask the person who programs your child into classes. Talk about the appropriateness of that teacher for your child rather than how good the teacher is. Limit your requests to perhaps one teacher a year.

In high school, students often self-program, making it easy to get the teachers of choice. If necessary, remind your child not to squander this opportunity—making the right choices can benefit him more than almost any single move he will make in high school. Choosing the right teachers means greater learning, more interesting classes, and the right amount of work.

In many schools, the most popular teachers' classes fill up fast. To avoid being closed out, encourage your child to volunteer to work at registration—registration volunteers usually get first crack at teacher choices.

Getting Your Child In

If easy alternatives such as self-scheduling aren't available, the next question is, "How do I get my child assigned to the teacher of my choice?"

In every locality we surveyed from coast to coast, we found some parents who got their requests for a specific teacher granted while other parents in the same community were unsuccessful. We asked principals to describe both situations and to explain the reasons for their decisions. We also spoke with parents who were successful and those who were unsuccessful in getting their requests granted. The following summarizes their experiences.

For starters, they widely agreed that a key to getting your request granted is asking at the right time. As mentioned earlier, the best time to ask is during the few days before the school year starts. By that time, the principal knows the teaching assignments yet can easily move your child from one class to another.

Most principals and parents also agree that what often makes the difference is not school or district policy, but how the parent makes the request. Most important, is making the request tactfully. All parents know they should be tactful, yet their dissatisfaction with the child's current teacher can make them lose their diplomatic demeanor.

Principals reported that parents typically start the conversation cordially but if the principal doesn't immediately agree, they can quickly disintegrate: "Mrs. Jackson is a horror. If you don't place my child with Mrs. Magnapede, I'll go to the superintendent!" Principals rarely accede to such threats because they know that higher-ups are reluctant to overrule the principal on such a small matter—the relationship between the principal and his bosses is too important to sacrifice for one child's class placement.

The principals also stressed that parents should never say that one teacher is better than another, only that one is better suited to meet the child's needs. Contrast the following two parents' requests.

Parent 1: I'd really appreciate it if you could place Chris with Mr. Wilens next year. He really is a fine teacher.

Parent 2: As you know, I visited two fifth-grade classes last week. From what little I know about education, I think that Seth would profit from Mr. Wilens's style of teaching and they would get along well together. Equally important, since there is no other male in our household, it would be wonderful if Seth could have a positive male figure in his life. So, I'm hoping Seth can get Mr. Wilens next year.

Parent 2 has a better chance of getting her child into Mr. Wilens's class because she didn't imply that Mr. Wilens was better than the other teachers, which might force the principal to defend them; she simply tried to match teacher and child appropriately, a goal most principals share.

Another point made by the principals is that parents need to justify why they should be allowed to choose when not all parents can do so. A parent should remind the principal that he has never before requested a teacher or at least not for several years by saying, "I've never requested (or I've tried to avoid requesting) a teacher because I'm aware that it's not fair that I should be able to choose while other parents can't. But I'm particularly concerned this year because . . ."

Here are some possible becauses:

1. My child had an unsuccessful school year this year.

2. My child is going through a particularly sensitive time now because his father has been ill (or I've just separated from my husband, his grandmother with whom he was close has died, etc.).

3. My child has been looking forward to having Mrs. Magnapede because his older brother had her and always talked about how much he enjoyed her class. [Add any other reasons why your child would particularly want to be in her class.] Also, her knowing my other son might help her in working with my child.

4. I observed Mrs. Magnapede teaching math and saw how clearly she explained math concepts. Johnny has been struggling this year in math and could really benefit from a year with Mrs. Magnapede.

5. My child is in the gifted program, but this year there hasn't seemed to have been much of a program in his class. I observed Mrs. Magnapede do some wonderfully creative things with her gifted students. I just think my son's needs and Mrs. Magnapede's strengths seem well matched.

6. I saw Mrs. Magnapede's class and I'm concerned that her phonic reading approach wouldn't work well with my

child. He's just getting the hang of reading and I'd hate to see him get a teacher who does lots of phonics.

7. If you're convinced that the principal knows Mrs. Malapede is a poor teacher, you may want to simply say, "I just don't think Mrs. Malapede would be right for my child."

A supporting letter from a school psychologist or other educator, preferably with a doctorate, or even from your pediatrician, often carries weight; schools don't want to risk a lawsuit by not following an expert's prescription.

Of course, there are no guarantees. Obstacles can and do arise, which only sometimes can be overcome by creativity or tactful persistence:

- The principal tells you that your child has already been irrevocably placed in Mrs. Malapede's class.

- The teacher you selected takes a maternity leave at the last minute.

- The teacher you selected for your bright child will be teaching a slower class.

- The principal says, "I honored your request the last two years. It's getting a little unfair." (The lesson to be learned here is that if you don't have a strong preference, don't request a teacher at all. That way, you may have some chits to use when you do have a preference.)

- The principal says, "I'd really like to grant your request, but if I did, I'd have to honor everybody's and I can't do that." (To avoid such a principal, we recommend, in Chapter 9, that in choosing your child's school, you ask the principal how much input you'll have in choosing your child's teacher.)

Think about how you feel when you walk out of a bad movie. And that's only two miserable hours. Now, compare that with how your child would feel if he had a bad teacher six hours a day, five days a week, for 180 days. Choosing your child's teacher once or twice in elementary school and occasionally in secondary school takes only a few hours of your time, yet can make your child's school years so much happier and more successful. In our view, it is the second most time-effective thing you can ever do for your child. The first? Choosing your child's school, the topic of the next chapter.

CHAPTER NINE

How to Decide If a School Is Right for Your Child

*I get nervous just going to the regular parent-teacher
conferences. Just walking into the school makes me feel
like I'm twelve years old and in the sixth grade again.
How can a twelve-year-old rate a school?*

A PUBLIC SCHOOL PARENT

Are you happy with your child's public school? Or do you
sometimes wonder:

- My child is ready to start kindergarten, and I'm not sure I want to send him to the local public school.

- My child's public school may be okay, but I'm not really sure.

- My child just graduated from elementary (or junior high) school, and I'm not sure I want to send him to the local junior (or senior) high school.

- We're moving and I'd like to find a place with a good public school.

- I'm shelling out big bucks every year for private school, and I wonder if I'm getting my money's worth. Wouldn't it be great if my child could get as good an education in a public school?

If you've ever harbored any of these thoughts, the following pages are for you. They will teach you how to competently decide if a school is right for your child. If the school isn't what it should be, you'll learn how to find and get your child into a better one—few parents realize that with a little know-how, they can legally get their children into a public school other than the regular district-assigned one. Finally, we suggest potent ways for parents to improve the school their child ends up attending.

The Transportation Problem

Some parents reject the idea of sending their child to a school other than the local one because of the transportation difficulties. In fact, the problem can often be alleviated by a parent driving, a carpool, public transit, student use of bicycle or moped, or a more creative solution. For example, one parent placed a classified ad in a community newspaper and quickly received a phone call from a commuter who was glad to have the company for her drive to and from work. Another parent got her child in a vanpool. A third parent obtained the addresses of the teachers at her child's school and called the one who lived closest to them. The teacher agreed to drive the child to and from school each day. In short, the transportation problem may not be as significant as it may first appear.

Why a Parent Would Spend More Time Choosing a Car Than a School

If you need a new automobile and your neighbor raves about her Fiat, do you run right out and buy a Fiat? Most new car buyers visit a few car dealers, compare features of various models, take test drives, even read *Consumer Reports*, and then shop for price.

Many parents choose their child's school less carefully than they choose a car, not because they're unconcerned, but because they believe they have no choice, or that they can rely on hearsay. Unfortunately, particularly in judging a school, hearsay can be wrong:

Linda: Hi, Sue. This is Linda, next door. I understand you got your son into Trendy School. What do you think of it?

Sue: I like it. And so do most of the other people I've talked with. It's got nice kids and the place seems pretty peaceful. The buildings are modern, the grounds are well maintained and they've recently carpeted the whole school. Also, I just went to back-to-school night and was impressed. My child's teacher described her program and it sounded very good. The classroom, in fact every classroom I peeked into, was immaculate and cheery. I also had a chance to talk with the principal and some other teachers during the coffee hour. They were friendly and sounded like they knew what they were talking about. Overall, my guess is that Trendy is a good school.

This may sound convincing. It's understandable that, if your child is in a school you've heard good things about, and your child isn't screaming bloody murder, you don't feel pressed to check it out firsthand. Unfortunately, choosing a school based on hearsay is risky. Many of the factors the public uses to judge a school just aren't valid.

Take for example, Sue's reasons for believing Trendy was a good school. None of them proves that the school is providing a good education. Some schools with nice kids and quiet classrooms don't provide good education. Attractive facilities are nice, but they don't teach Junior how to read. Back-to-school night is little more than a public relations event—choosing a school based on back-to-school night is like using a TV commercial to choose your new car.

We've seen many children receive a mediocre education in a school with a good reputation. Even if a school's reputation is deserved, it doesn't mean it's the right school for your child. Toyota may have a deservedly good reputation, but it may not be the right car for you.

Yet, based largely on a school's reputation, parents may move into that school's attendance area, make major efforts to maneuver their child into the school, or even justify annual kilodollar expenditures for private school. Shouldn't you evaluate your child's school or choose a new one at least as carefully as you choose a car?

But choosing a school based on reputation is better than not choosing at all. Some parents don't choose because they think they don't have a choice. Private school is not an option for them, and they believe their child can only attend the local public school. This is often untrue. For years, parents in-the-know have been getting their children into public schools other than their local one. Chapter 10 will show you how they do it.

Other parents just accept the assigned public school because they're uncomfortable with the idea of reviewing and choosing a school. One parent said, "I get nervous just going to the regular parent-teacher conferences. Just walking into the school makes me feel like I'm twelve years old and in the sixth grade again. How can a twelve-year-old rate a school?"

Still other parents don't check out their child's school because they don't know what to look for. They allow themselves to believe the school is probably fine, but regrettably, some schools are *not* fine. Taking potluck with your child's school is almost like betting your child's welfare on a roll of the dice.

The Price of Not Choosing

We've seen many children suffer because they attended the wrong school. Chris is an example. We met Chris and his mother, Kate, when he was in the sixth grade. They recounted, in great detail, Chris's sad history at his local elementary school. This is Kate's story:

> When Chris was five, I enrolled him in kindergarten at the local elementary school, King Elementary. He was so excited that first day; he marched into school without looking back once. Chris had always been a bright child and we've tried to give him an enriching home life, so, I drove away that first day, confident everything would be fine.
>
> As you may have guessed, I was wrong. Everything seemed all right for the first few months. After Christmas, Chris didn't seem anxious to go back to school, but I figured that's normal; the novelty of school was beginning to wear off. After all, I wasn't always so enthusiastic about school when I was a child. But I started to worry when I noticed that Chris seemed sad every time we talked about school. His typical response to, "What did you do in school today?" was an apathetic, "Nothin', Mom." I sensed trouble.
>
> I went in to see his teacher. She also had noticed that Chris seemed unhappy about school and thought that it was be-

cause he found the work too easy. When I asked if she could give him harder work, she said that she would try, but couldn't really be expected to develop an individualized program just for Chris.

I asked if Chris might be able to work with the special teacher he had mentioned to me. As though shocked at the thought, she answered, "Oh, no. That teacher can only work with the Chapter I [low achieving] children. It's against the law for Chris to use the Chapter I materials by himself, even if they're just sitting around unused."

I asked the teacher what services are available for a child like Chris. A little embarrassed, she said that there weren't any and quickly ended the conference, assuring me that there was nothing to worry about: "A bright boy like Chris will do fine in the long run." I left, angry and worried.

Things got worse. Chris told me that he didn't want to answer questions in class any more because the other kids didn't, and when he did, they called him "brown nose." Whereas Chris previously had little interest in TV other than "The Electric Company," he now had to watch "The A Team" and "The Dukes of Hazzard." "Mom, everyone watches those shows.'The Electric Company' is for sissies".

In subsequent years, Chris continued to be bored in school, one reason being that the school's classes were not grouped by ability. He complained that his teachers had to explain the same thing umpteen times until everyone understood it. There were no aides or parent volunteers to help meet Chris's needs, as there are in other schools. The few aides or parent volunteers were always assigned to help the students who needed remediation.

Finally, in third grade, Kate found a teacher she thought would be good for Chris. But the principal said that he didn't honor parent requests for teachers. As chance would have it, Chris got the other third-grade teacher.

Year after year, Chris basically just went through the motions. We heard all this when Chris was in the sixth grade, still at King School, bored, achieving no better than average, with some friends we wouldn't want our daughter spending time with.

While Kate continued to be concerned, she never really did much to improve the situation. We can't help but think that Chris would have been better off in another school. After all, he came to school with good potential—in kindergarten, he scored at the 80th percentile on the standardized test battery. But by the sixth grade, his scores had declined to near the 50th percentile. It would seem that King School had something to do with the decline.

Of course, not every school-placement decision will profoundly affect a child. In your community, the differences between schools may not be so extreme, but the school your child attends can make a significant difference. It certainly seems worth the short time it takes to check out your child's school, if for reassurance alone. If your child attends the wrong school, you'll probably spend more time, emotional energy, and perhaps money trying to solve a problem that might readily have been prevented.

Choosing: First Steps

If you're already comfortably planted in your home with no desire to uproot, check out your child's school first. It may be just fine. If he's attending private school, you may want to check out your local public school for comparison. Could you be saving thousands of dollars every year?

If you're looking for a new school, you may want to visit two or three schools before choosing. But, which ones? Call your local school district office and ask for the names of schools that have:

- more than one teacher per grade level (you don't have much choice if there's only one teacher per grade level);

- any special program your child needs: special education, a gifted program, an athletic team, etc;

- the "right" philosophy: college preparatory, back-to-basics, open classroom, competitive, noncompetitive, etc;

- feasible transportation.

Ask if any of the schools are "open-enrollment" schools. Any students residing in the district may attend these schools without obtaining special permission. If the district office suggests more than three schools, you can narrow the list by speaking with a respected parent or a substitute teacher who has taught in the schools you're considering. The district office may give you a substitute's name and phone number, but if not, leave a message for the substitute to call you.

Do not be dismayed if you are told that there are no open-enrollment schools in your district, or that there are some but they are overcrowded. The next chapter explains how you can get your child into the school of your choice, whether it is an open-enrollment school or not, overcrowded or not. For now, though, keep your focus on finding a school that is right for your child.

If you're unable to come up with potentially acceptable schools within your local district, you may want to investigate out-of-district public schools. Chapter 10 suggests a procedure for getting your child admitted to an out-of-district public school. However, an out-of-district public school should be a last resort because it typically is difficult to obtain the necessary permissions.

If you're moving and have some latitude in choosing your location, you may want to choose a school first and then find a place to live in that school's attendance area, so you don't have to apply for special permission.

How to Grade a School

You can use the School Report Card to help you grade your child's school or select a new one. Each School Report Card item has been identified by research and experience as a crucial characteristic of an excellent school that a noneducator can observe in one school visit.

The School Report Card is divided into two parts: yes/no questions to ask the principal (or a counselor at a junior or senior high school), and things to look for as you walk through the school and visit a few classrooms in action. You can't learn everything about a school in one visit, but you'll learn enough to decide if the school is right for your child.

For parents who prefer an even simpler way to judge, there's the short form of the School Report Card which contains fewer items to ask the principal and to look for in a school visit. While the regular version is recommended, the short form also provides a reasonable basis for judging a school.

Some parents are concerned that the principal won't let them visit classrooms. There's certainly no problem if you can visit during a school's Open School Days, and during other times, most principals are usually quite willing to cooperate with a politely inquiring parent. Even if the principal doesn't allow you to visit classrooms, you can learn a lot from walking through the halls, glancing into classrooms and chatting with a few students. You might also ask the questions on the School Report Card of a parent or two who are active at the school.

Making an Appointment

If you can't visit during Open School Days, your next step is to make an appointment to see the principal (or counselor or dean if you are looking into a junior or senior high school). This may not be quite as easy as it sounds but here's a good approach:

Secretary: Good morning, Kennedy School.

Parent: Hello. This is Mary Smith, a parent. I'd like to meet with the principal for about ten minutes, just after one of your recesses.

Secretary: May I ask what it's in reference to?

Parent: I have a few questions I'd like to ask the principal about the school.

Secretary: Perhaps I can answer them for you.

Parent: Thank you, but I really think I need to speak with the principal.

Secretary: All right. How's Wednesday at 12:15?

Parent: That's fine. Thank you.

This parent did a number of desirable things in her phone call:

1. She made an appointment rather than just dropping in on the principal.

2. She requested her appointment at a time which would allow her to observe the students at recess.

3. She let the secretary know that she will only take about ten minutes of the principal's time.

4. She explained her reason for wanting to speak with the principal in a way that would not cause concern.

5. When the secretary wanted to answer the parent's questions, the parent remained polite yet firm about needing to speak with the principal without having to go into a long explanation.

Me, Interview a Principal?

Most job seekers would agree that employers have a right to interview before hiring, even though interviews are often uncomfortable. Employers maintain, and the courts have upheld, that their interests are important enough to give them the right to ask even personal questions.

When you ask the principal the questions on the School Report Card, you are essentially interviewing him or her for the job of educator of your child. When you consider that this "hiring situation" involves the welfare of your child—the questions on the School Report Card seem tame.

Indeed, most parents find the principal willing to answer the questions on the School Report Card candidly. The process usually amounts to an informative and cordial ten- to fifteen-minute chat with the school official gaining a measure of respect for the parent.

The key to a cordial and candid interview with the principal is the way you explain why you're asking him the questions. Put yourself in the principal's shoes. If a parent asked you the kind of questions about his school that only a knowledgeable educator would know to ask, wouldn't you feel a bit uncomfortable? Wouldn't you need some reassurance that the parent wasn't a gadfly from the press, spy from the school board, or someone otherwise looking to cause trouble?

We showed Justine how to use the School Report Card. After trying it, she said that the procedure didn't work because the principal refused to let her visit classrooms. When she described her meeting with the principal, we understood why:

Principal: Come in.

Justine: Thank you. Schools sure are noisier than when I was a child. Anyway, I understand I have the right to inspect my child's school, and so I want to ask you a few questions? (She asks the questions from the School Report Card.) Now, might I check out a few teachers' classrooms?

Principal: I'd like to let you, but I don't like to disrupt instruction any more than I absolutely have to. I hope you understand.

Justine committed four errors that may have discouraged the principal from cooperating with her.

1. She started right off with an implied criticism of the school's noise level, an action not likely to encourage the principal's cooperation.

2. She did nothing to allay any concerns about her motives.

3. By saying, "I understand I have the right to inspect my child's school," she implicitly threatened to go over the principal's head if he didn't cooperate. Most principals are aware that parents are unlikely to do so, and even if they do, the principal probably won't be overruled on such a small issue. Thus, such threats rarely scare a principal. They merely make him or her less likely to cooperate.

4. Justine's request to "check out a few teachers" implied that they may not be doing well. Principals are aware of weaknesses in some teachers, but are unlikely to want to help a parent discover them.

In contrast, consider another parent's approach:

Principal: Come in.

Pat: I appreciate your taking the time to see me. I know how busy principals are. I've always believed in public education but all the media reports about problems in the public schools have got us a bit worried. I haven't heard unfavorable things about your school, but my child is (may become) a student here and my husband and I feel the need for some reassurance that our child won't get short-changed if we keep him in public school.

I've been reading a book called *How to Get a "Private School" Education in a Public School*. It says that you can gain a lot of reassurance by asking the principal a few questions. That's why I'm here. Might I ask them of you? (She asks the School Report Card questions.)

The book also suggests that parents can get a feel for the public schools by visiting a few classrooms. Might I briefly visit two or three that my child might eventually be in? I'll be as unobtrusive as possible.

In all dealings with the school, if you remember the difference between Justine's and Pat's approaches, you'll have a big advantage. The principal or counselor will usually be willing to answer your questions and allow you to visit classrooms although you may be asked to do so on another day so there is time to inform the teachers.

If Pat's general approach is followed, interviewing the principal can be simple, even for a timid soul. Nevertheless, some parents may still feel uncomfortable about it. If only some of the questions make you queasy, you may want to just ask those that don't. If nine questions seems too many, just ask the five on the short form. At a junior or senior high school, you only need ask three. You can even choose to skip the question part of the School Report Card altogether and judge the school only on the visit. Doing this, you'll still be better able to judge if a school is right for your child than if you judge on reputation alone.

Other parents feel comfortable about asking the principal questions, but believe that they can't count on honest responses. Naturally, it would be unrealistic to expect a school official to lambast his own school, but the questions on the School Report Card don't require him to—they are relatively objective, not requiring him to judge his school as good or bad.

So, assuming you've decided to ask the principal at least some of the questions on the School Report Card, there you are in his office, ready to find out if his school is the right one for your child. You've brought with you the "shopping list," the abbreviated list of the School Report Card items, to remind you of what to ask the principal and what to look for in your school visit.

The rest of this chapter essentially is a short course on the effective school. So, in addition to helping you decide if a school is right for your child, it can make you a more effective member of a school or school district committee.

What to Ask the Principal

In junior or senior high schools, ask only questions 7, 8, and 9, and ask them of a counselor, not the principal. (The short form items are starred.)

*Question 1: How many teachers are there at each grade?

Some teachers will be better for your child than others, perhaps one who is male or female, firm or permissive, better with fast learners or with slow ones. Some teachers are simply better than others. So, you need a school with a choice of teachers at each grade level. The more teachers at each grade level, the more likely you are to find one who is right for your child. Also, the chances of a principal's approving the teacher you choose are better when he's juggling students among five teachers than between two.

*Question 2: Do many aides and parents work in the classrooms?

It's a plus if your child attends a school with many aides and parents working in classrooms. They can provide kids with extra help or TLC, making a large class seem a little smaller. They can also take care of nonteaching tasks to free the teacher to work with students. Finally, volunteering parents demonstrate that they value education—kids take cues from parents.

Aides and parent volunteers can even enrich instruction by giving presentations on their work experiences or avocations. One parent, a newspaper reporter, on hearing that his child's class was learning about ancient Rome, led the class in creating "The Roman Times" newspaper.

An active Parent-Teacher Association can also benefit a school. For example, some PTA's collect considerable sums of money which are used to provide important school programs like homework helplines and mini-courses for the gifted.

Question 3: Is there a schoolwide system of student awards?

We all respond to incentives. How many people would work if they didn't get paid? Children needs incentives, too. We ask them to work diligently in school, and what are their incentives? The joys of learning, a report card issued a few times a year, and a vague promise that their efforts will pay off in some long run, years away. These incentives are insufficient for many students.

Good schools give many awards to provide additional incentives: lunch with the principal for service to the school, honor roll certificates for scholarship, coupons donated by burger chains for improved report cards, a school trip to an amusement part for a B average or better, etc.

Leyva Junior High School in San Jose, California, has a wonderfully ingenious and elaborate system. A Bravo is a card emblazoned, "Bulldog Bravo to _____ for showing a spirit of cooperation, lending a hand, behaving maturely, and having consideration for others." Bravos are awarded liberally, and are good in trade at the student store and in quantity, earn a mention on the morning announcements. Lunchtime contests in anything from cheerleading to doughnut eating also bring Bravos to the winners. We wish we could have gone to Leyva.

Remember how you felt when you received an award, especially one given in public, either on the job, while working for an organization, or when you were a student? Imagine how a student feels when he receives one, especially on the school stage in front of all the students. Not only is it a proud moment and a fond memory, it also probably makes him want to keep up the good work. Your child may not be an honor student or the school's hope for All-American, but awards are important to everybody.

William used to be in a regular class, but no matter how hard he tried, he just couldn't keep up. Finally, he was put in room 14, the class for the educationally handicapped. William knew he belonged there, but it still hurt to line up with the "retards" when he saw his old class just across the way.

One day after school, William stopped by his former first-grade teacher's class. It was his way of consoling himself. "At least, I used to be in a regular class."

"Hi, Mrs. Chapman. I figured I'd come by and say, hi."

"Hello, William. How are you?"

"Fine, how are you?"

"Fine, thank you."

After a bit more awkwardness, he excused himself, even though he would have liked to stay longer. Just before he reached the door, he noticed a small rabbit in a cage. He stopped to look at it, and kept gazing at it for a full minute. Finally, Mrs. Chapman understood. She came over to William and said, "That's Gomer. You know, we need someone reliable to take care of him. By any chance, would you have time every day after school to feed him and clean his cage?"

William nodded, his eyes welling up with pride and happiness. He never missed a day. When he was absent, he called his best friend in his special education class to take care of Gomer.

At the end of the year, the entire school met in the auditorium for an awards assembly. Each honoree proudly marched on stage to claim an award. Somewhere in the middle of the long list, came the announcement, "William Donovan—service award." Too scared to smile and covered with goosebumps, William rose from his seat. His classmates, in both the special and his old regular class, whispered, and then clapped.

All children can benefit from the knowledge that with effort, they can earn an award.

Question 4: Is there a schoolwide homework policy?

One of education's few truisms is simply that the more time students spend learning, the more they'll learn. Giving homework is any easy way to increase learning time. Homework also provides time to do research projects and to practice what was learned in school. It's particularly important in math, grammar, spelling, and foreign language. It's not possible to do everything in the classroom, so a schoolwide policy requiring a moderate amount of meaningful homework is a plus. Some students may disagree.

Question 5: Does the school have a formal curriculum?

"Curriculum" refers to the content and methods of instruction. Every school has some sort of curriculum but the quality varies widely. So, the question you're really interested in is, "Does the school have a *good* curriculum?" But, you can't ask this question because it would put the principal in an uncomfortable position. So, instead, simply ask, "Does the school have a formal curriculum?" and let him or her explain or show it to you.

Inadequate curricula are merely vague statements of philosophy offering clichés about the importance of citizenship and basic skills. These have no impact on what goes on in the classroom. Teachers in schools with such a curriculum have to develop or select their own, a task they may not be trained to do, and a task that certainly takes time away from other necessary activities.

Better schools use curricula that are professionally developed, detailed cookbooks for teaching just about everything from kindergarten arithmetic to twelfth grade career education, so teachers don't have to reinvent the wheel each time they teach something. The creative teacher can adapt the curriculum as needed, but starts out with a well-thought-out foundation on which to superimpose his creativity. A cookbook can help even the most creative chef.

Question 6: Are there specialist teachers at the school?

We live in the age of specialization and most of us prefer it. If we have lousy gums, most people would rather see a periodontist rather than our all-purpose driller. If some drunk runs a red light and smashes our car, most of us would choose a personal injury attorney rather than a general lawyer.

Students also profit from specialists, teachers who go from class to class for lessons, teaching in their area of expertise. Without them, some subjects often would be taught poorly or not at all: gifted education, music, art, physical education, computers, and, perhaps most significantly, science. Unless there is a specialist, many elementary school children receive only the barest science program because few elementary school teachers have a strong science background.

Question 7: Are classes grouped by student ability?

Although there is controversy on this issue, most evidence suggests that classes should be grouped by student ability, at

153

least for some academic subjects. A review of fifty-two separate studies on the effects of ability grouping concluded that "in more than 70 percent of these studies, students from the grouped classes outperformed students from the ungrouped classes by at least a small amount." Student attitudes toward the subject being taught and toward school in general were higher in ability-grouped classes. While the benefits of ability-grouped classes were particularly great for above-average students, ability grouping had a small positive or zero effect for average or low ability students. In short, the evidence suggests that ability grouping helps many students, and hurts none.[1]

These research results aren't surprising. Most teachers aim their lessons at the middle of the class. In an ability-grouped class, no child is far from that middle, but in a mixed ability class, the greater disparity usually leaves the bright children bored and the slow ones behind. To compensate, teachers of mixed classes have to resort to "individualized instruction," an enticing concept but usually a practical disaster, as will be explained later.

A slow child's self-esteem usually suffers in mixed classes since, no matter how hard he tries, he always does worse than his much more able classmates. He's reminded of his inferiority with every test, every assignment, and every question the teacher asks the class. These constant reminders are likely to be far more damaging to a child's self-esteem than being placed in a slower paced class where he can, on a regular basis, find appropriately leveled instruction.

A bright child also fares poorly in a mixed class. Rena spends much of her school day waiting: waiting while the teacher explains the concept for the third time, waiting for a slow child to finish stumbling through the paragraph, waiting for the slow children to ask and for the teacher to answer myriad low-level questions. The rationale that bright students should help the slower ones is unfair—every child, bright or slow, is entitled to an appropriately leveled education. The "bright-tutoring-the-slow" concept is a fast way to reduce bright students to the

[1]Kulik, J. & Kulik, C. Effects of Ability Grouping on Student Achievement. *Equity & Excellence*, 23(1-2), 22-29, 1987.

lowest common denominator. Yet it is the foundation of education's newest fad, "cooperative learning."

An example from adult life may make clearer the advantages of ability-grouped classes. Imagine you were taking a Chinese cooking class at your local adult school. You go to the first class with fantasies of serving your amazed family an impressive and unpronounceable banquet and with more realistic hopes of making an acceptable chow mein.

By the end of the first class, your hopes, not to mention your fantasies, have been stir-fried away. Most of the people in the class were already quite at home around a wok, and the instruction was understandably, aimed at this majority. As a result, their offerings were magnificent, yours were burnt. The problem: people of disparate abilities in the same class, different dishes in the same wok.

If you, as an adult, couldn't profit from such a situation, imagine your child in too difficult a class. More importantly, if you don't learn Chinese cooking, you can always go back to meat and potatoes. But if your child doesn't learn to read, what can he do?

The problem is equally serious for the advanced student. In our example, a professional Chinese chef would learn little from an intermediate class. An effective answer is simply to assign students to classes by ability.

Question 8: Would I have any input in choosing my child's teachers?

Having the right teachers, or at least avoiding the wrong ones, is crucial to ensuring a good education for your child. Some principals welcome parent requests while others discourage them. So, it's important to find out how much input the principal will allow you.

Question 9: Does the school do well on standardized achievement tests?

Despite the criticisms often leveled at standardized achievement tests, they are reasonably good indicators of a school's overall academic achievement, at least in terms of traditional academic skills. Average percentile ranks above 60 or so are a plus if your child is an average or above-average student.

You may want a low-achieving child to attend a school with slightly lower achievement test scores (40th to 60th percentiles), because if the school has many children achieving near your child's levels, your child may have a better chance of receiving appropriate instruction and maintaining good self-esteem.

After you've finished asking the principal these questions, thanked him, told him that the book you've been reading suggested that you can get a feel for the school by visiting a few classrooms, and obtained the room numbers and directions to a few classes that your child might eventually be in, you're ready to take a look at the school.

A Firsthand Look at the School

The visit items from the School Report Card can help you find out the truth, firsthand: is your neighbor correct in calling the school, "wonderful"? How valid are those glowing reports the principal and teachers gave at PTA meetings and at Back-to-School night? Are the children at this school likely to lead your little angel down the road to perdition? Are the media referring to this school when they say the public schools are dying?

Most parents not only find their school visit informative, but also enjoyable. One parent, Mrs. Jorgensen, told us about a wonderful experience she had. When she walked into one classroom, the teacher asked pleasantly, "In our class, we prefer participants to observers. How would you like to read this story to the Robins?" As soon as Mrs. Jorgensen nodded, six youngsters popped up and, like magic, were seated in a semicircle on a rug in the back of the room. Mrs. Jorgensen read, *The Giving Tree* to six entranced seven-year-olds. No sooner did she finish than the teacher said, "Time for art. Today, we're going to make stained glass windows. You, too, Mrs. Jorgensen." And just like the rest of the class, Mrs. Jorgensen made a stained glass window of colored glassine. Even though she was participating, she had plenty of opportunity to observe. Although not all parents find their school visits quite as enjoyable, most leave school having had a pleasant as well as informative experience.

Some parents, however, do not look forward to visiting classrooms, at least during times other than Open School Days. They are uncomfortable barging in on classes in session, with the students wondering who the strange adult is. At the risk of sounding like a guilt-provoking parent, so you'll be a little uncomfortable. Isn't your child's welfare worth it?

Besides, your visit will probably be less uncomfortable than you may think. In days of yore, parents were indeed rare visitors to classrooms, except on Open School Days, but that has changed with today's increasing emphasis on community involvement in schools. When you walk into a classroom, you'll be viewed as only a minor novelty. Remember, too, that you won't be walking into classes at random. The principal will have told you which teachers to visit, and you can be sure that he or she only suggested teachers who wouldn't mind your presence.

Some parents are reluctant to visit because they fear that a brief look may not permit a valid judgement. This concern is understandable. But actually, you'll learn more from a brief observation focused on the School Report Card items than from hours of unfocused looking. Briefly visiting three classrooms and watching a recess may not enable you to observe all the items on the School Report Card, but will give you enough information to decide if a school is right for your child. You'll certainly make a better decision than if you decide on hearsay.

Still other parents feel that visiting classrooms may give an inaccurate impression of the school because the teachers and the students will be on their best behavior. Indeed, you are not a fly on the wall when you visit. Common sense would suggest that despite being nervous in front of an inspector, teacher and students will be somewhat better than if you weren't there.

I would have agreed, until I supervised student teachers. Even though the student teacher's course grade, and even her teaching credential hung in the balance, I sometimes saw poorly behaved students and pathetic teaching. One time, a student teacher showed a film while I was there to observe. Fifteen minutes remained in the period after the film was over, but she had planned nothing for the class to do, even though she knew I was coming. The least she could have done was ask for student reactions to the film, but, what did she do? She showed the film backward! Such incidents have convinced me that a parent can observe a teacher without expecting a command performance that ends as soon as the parent leaves the classroom. Besides, even if the teacher and students try harder when being observed, that little extra usually doesn't change the overall picture.

Despite all reassurances, a few parents do the visit part of the School Report Card without entering a classroom. They just walk through the halls, glance into a few classrooms and spend a few minutes watching recess. Even this can be very informative. Look especially to see if most students appear to be working hard, yet contentedly.

Assuming you've decided to visit classrooms, you probably still have a few questions. Here are the common ones:

- **"Which classrooms should I visit?"** Ask the principal to suggest a few classrooms to which your child might eventually be assigned. If there is a teacher you are interested in—whether for good or bad—and the principal doesn't include her, you might add, "Could I also visit Mrs. Malapede's class? I've heard her name mentioned by other parents."

- **"How do I find the classrooms?"** Just ask the principal. Many schools have maps you can use. If you can't find the second class on your own, ask a student to direct you. Kids feel proud when they can help grown-ups.

- **"Do I just walk right in?"** Sure, unless the teacher seems terribly involved in something that will only last a few moments, in which case you might just wait by the door for an opportune moment. If the class is taking a test or watching a movie, you might visit another class first.

- **"What should I say when I walk in?"** You might say something like, "Hi, I'm Mrs. Smith, a parent. The principal said it was all right if I briefly visited [don't say, "observed"] a few classes. He suggested yours. I hope you don't mind."

- **"What do I do next?"** Sometimes, the teacher will direct you to a seat, but often you'll be invited to walk around. Do whatever feels comfortable. Walking around gives you the opportunity to see more students and the work they're doing. But if you prefer to sit, you might choose a spot where you can see as many children's faces as possible—they can be telling.

Next, try to pick out one or two children who seem similar to your own child in ability and/or disposition; for example, the hand-raiser versus the cut-up, the brain versus the boggled. Then interpret each School Report Card item as it pertains to them. For example, interpret item 2, "Are students working hard yet contentedly?" as, "Are students *like my child* working hard yet contentedly?" This will help you decide whether the school is right for your child and not just good in general.

- **"How do I remember the School Report Card items?"** You shouldn't take the actual School Report Card with you—an $8^1/_2$ x 11-inch rating sheet just doesn't create the right impression. So, just bring the tiny "shopping list," an abbreviated listing of the items, presented on page 169.

- **"When do I leave?"** If you've watched the class in action for fifteen to twenty minutes, you've probably seen enough. Wait for an opportune moment, whisper a quick "thank you," wave goodbye, and leave. However, if it's clear that the class is about to end, for example, just before recess, you might wait until the students are dismissed, and, as a courtesy, thank the teacher more formally. This also may give you an opportunity to get to know him better.

What to Look for in Your School Visit

Here are the visit items on the School Report Card, expressed as yes/no questions, each with an explanation of why it's important, and how you can answer it in your brief visit. Questions 1, 2, 4, 6, and 8 are taken directly from the Teacher Report Card and were discussed in Chapter 8. So they will be presented here without comment.

Question 1: Are the student spending most of their time on worthwhile activities? (See page 126.)

Question 2: Are most students working hard yet contentedly? (See pages 125 and 127.)

Question 3: Do teachers spend a lot of time interactively teaching groups of one-third of the class or larger? (See pages 128-129.)

Behind this rather complicated question lies a rather simple concept. But it does require some explanation.

If you've been aware of educational trends over the last twenty years, you've probably heard about "individualized instruction." Who would disagree with individualized instruction? It's almost like disagreeing with motherhood. And it was largely this intuitive appeal that made individualized instruction the rage in many classrooms in the '70s and keeps it popular today. The truth is that individualization is great—for a class of five.

However, the reality of thirty students per class forces the teacher to make significant compromises when individualizing instruction. For example, in order for each child to work at his own level and pace, the teacher must basically stop teaching the class and spend most of his time developing and correcting individualized assignments. What this means, is that most students are teaching themselves—sink or swim.

Thus, these teachers abdicate their role as teachers to become monitors of as many as thirty programs simultaneously going on at thirty desks. They can often be seen earnestly racing from desk to desk putting out fires—explaining, cajoling, enriching, with each child receiving teacher-directed instruction about $1/_{30}$th of the time. If a student doesn't understand his work, he is typically left to complete it, making the same errors again and again until the teacher has time to get to him.

Another weakness of individualized instruction is that for less than motivated students, working at their own pace really means, "as slowly as they can get away with." And with one teacher being pulled in thirty directions at once, the unmotivated child can usually get away with some pretty slow work. For these reasons, individualized classrooms are often chaotic and inefficient.

Theoretically, we as adults could do all our learning out of books, at our own pace. Yet we typically choose to attend college, adult school, or workshops because we realize that having a teacher helps us learn more. How many of us could learn without a teacher, using only texts and worksheets every day of the school year, year after year? Yet this is essentially what teachers ask children to do when they adopt what is so seductively called "individualized instruction."

Many experts on school effectiveness now agree that effective schools have teachers who spend at least half of classtime on large-group (one-third or more of the class) activities, especially interactive ones like discussions, demonstrations, and simulations, rather than lectures. Independent seatwork should be used primarily to reinforce teacher-taught material; it should not be the predominant means of instruction.

Of course, even if large-group teacher-directed instruction predominates at the school, during your visit to any one classroom, the class may be doing independent seatwork; it is a part of all classrooms. But, by visiting a few classrooms and noticing other classes as you walk from room to room, you can get an idea of the school norm.

Question 4: Do teachers address individual student needs?

After criticizing so-called individualized instruction, it may seem contradictory to recommend that you look for a school in which the teachers address individual student needs. But it isn't. There are many ways a teacher can address individual needs even when teaching a lesson to the entire class. These were described in Chapter 8 (See pages 127-128.)

Question 5: Are many aides and parents working in the classrooms?

Aides and parents in the classroom can greatly enrich a school. Look for them as you visit classrooms and notice other classes as you walk through the halls.

Question 6: Do the teachers seem to care about their students? (See pages 127-128.)

Question 7: Do the teachers praise appropriately?

If your boss or spouse praises the way you do something, you tend to keep doing it that way or even try to improve further. On the other hand, if you're criticized, you often react negatively.

Although carefully couched constructive criticism can be valuable, it makes sense that praise should also generally work better than criticism with children. If David has been working hard to improve his cursive writing, a kind "Your S's are looking great. Do you think you can do as well with your T's?" will likely spur him on further than "Now practice your T's. They really need work."

Looking at teachers' use of praise is useful in judging a school, not only because of the power of praise, but because the amount of praise dispensed is an index of the school's atmosphere. If teachers are so burned out or if students are so bad that praise is rarely heard, you have learned something important about that school.

But praise is not always a plus. Praise given too frequently, when not specific, or not truly earned, ceases to be valued by students. Consider the situation in which Johnny has been in fine form as the class clown, constantly doing something to get a laugh. He finally runs out of material and relents for a moment. The teacher seizes the opportunity to compliment him, having learned in college that teachers should find things to praise in all students, and says, "You're a good boy, Johnny." If the teacher makes a habit of dispensing such praise, the students will quickly cease to value this teacher's praise and, eventually, the teacher himself.

Question 8: Are the teachers well educated in general and especially in the subject they teach? (See pages 129-130.)

Question 9: Are students orderly in the halls and during recess?

Watching students at recess and in the corridors can tell you a lot about a school. While, teasing, roughhousing, and even fighting occasionally occur at all schools, the more of this you see, the more concerned you should be. It not only indicates that the school's discipline system is weak, and that your child's safety may be in question, but also speaks poorly of the dominant values of the students at the school. (Identify yourself to the recess supervisor to reassure him that you're not there to kidnap one of the students.)

Question 10: Is the principal a good leader of the school?

A good principal makes a decisive difference in a school: setting high standards for the faculty and helping them to meet those standards. He or she is in firm control of the school, its discipline system as well as its administrative details, commanding the students' respect, and acting as a effective liaison between school and parents.

It's difficult to judge a principal in your first brief visit, but here are some qualities you might have the opportunity to notice.

- The principal's performance when you talked with her is probably your best indicator. Did her manner seem seem like it would inspire the respect of teachers and students? When you asked about the school's test scores and curriculum, were the documents readily available, or did she fumble around trying to find them?

- A good principal is highly visible. She has to spend a certain amount of time in the office but tries to stay in touch with the school by occasionally monitoring the student rush between periods, chatting with kids in the lunchroom, and, importantly, working with teachers in classrooms.

- A principal is an executive. As such, she must be respected and liked. Are interactions with teachers and students businesslike yet cordial? Is it obvious that they respect her, or do they openly display boredom, disinterest, and even insolence? Are such discourtesies, if they occur, handled with firmness and dignity?

Question 11: Is the physical plant adequate?

Inadequate buildings or landscaping usually reflect financial realities rather than lack of caring. Some wonderful schools reside in unattractive shells. So, don't heavily downgrade a school for inadequate facilities. It has been said that it is far better to have good teachers in wooden buildings than wooden teachers in good buildings.

On the other hand, some aspects of a school's physical plant are important. Beware if the doors on the bathroom stalls have been removed to discourage smokers and dopers.

See if classrooms are separated only by thin partitions that allow Room 6's spelling quiz to be accompanied by Room 8's music lesson.

Is the school riddled with broken windows or marred with graffiti and litter? These things convey to students that not only do some of their peers lack respect for the school, but that school officials don't care enough to make the school appear respectable.

Question 12: Do the school's books and equipment seem adequate?

Parents can be unduly impressed by a school's books and equipment. The essence of good schools lies in its students, teachers, and principal; no amount of fancy-covered texts, no amount of computers, can compensate for a school's inadequacies in its people. Nonetheless, a school should have adequate books and equipment. Here are some things to look for:

- Textbooks are much better than they were ten years ago. Not only is the content more current, but the presentation of the content is also improved. So, check if the textbooks look like they've been around since the Cuban missile crisis.

- Are kids sharing textbooks? Sharing books in class is bad enough. Eyes and neck are strained trying to read something at the next desk. A fast reader has to wait for his slower partner to turn the page. Sharing often leads to distraction: "Hey, the book is closer to your side. Put it in the middle." "No! You never put it in the middle." Even worse, shared books make it impossible for the teacher to assign homework in textbooks and makes it difficult for students to take texts home: "I've got to take it home. I have to catch up!" "No! You had it yesterday!" Besides, kids like having their own books, just "because."

- Televisions, video-tape recorders, slide projectors, overhead projectors, all add visual impact to lessons. Fancy equipment is no substitute for a good teacher, but judiciously used, like a fine spice, can add flavor.

- Computers impress many parents, but, too often, the hardware just sits around unused in classrooms. Are the covers gathering dust? Is the computer area so neat that it looks like it hasn't been visited since those Apples were planted?

Question 13: Is the school the regularly assigned public school?

Attending your regularly assigned public school has a number of advantages. First, getting your child to and from school is usually simpler (if the child doesn't live close enough to walk, the school district usually provides bus transportation). Second, a child tends to develop closer friendships if he attends school with the neighborhood children. Third, because of proximity, it's often easier for your child to take advantage of any school-sponsored after-school activities, not to mention the school library. Fourth, you don't need special permission for your child to attend the assigned school.

Question 14: Is the school convenient to before-or after-school activities?

You may find it important that your child's school be close to after-school activities (soccer practice, ballet lessons, or religion classes). Also, be aware of the locations of childcare facilities for before or after school.

Question 15: Are there any other factors to consider in judging this school?

Depending on your child's special needs or interests there may be other things you wish to consider: the elective-course offerings, a particularly active student government, newspaper or athletic program, avant-garde or traditional instruction, after-school childcare programs, an older sibling having attended there or, of course, your child's preference. Finally, you'll proba bly want to determine if there will be any extra costs involved in sending your child to the school.

Below is a listing of all the questions from the School Report Card and the condensed version "shopping list", to take with you on a school visit.

You can probably decide if the school is right for your child by using the School Report Card items solely as guidelines, but some parents prefer to "score" a school on the School Report Card items. For these parents, a simple scoring system has been included.

The School Report Card
Official Screening Instrument for the National Public School Awards

_____   _____
School   Date

Directions: Simply use the items as guidelines or circle the appropriate score for each question. The starred items are for the Short Form.

Questions Asked of the Principal
(For junior or senior high schools, usually see a counselor, and ask only questions 2, 8, and 9).

	Yes	Partially or Not Sure	No
★ 1. Are there at least three teachers per grade level?	12	6	0
★ 2. Are classes grouped by student ability?	12	6	0
★ 3. Do many aides and parents work in the classroom?	4	2	0
4. Are there specialist teachers at the school?	8	4	0
5. Is there a schoolwide system of student awards?	4	2	0
6. Is there a schoolwide homework policy?	4	2	0
7. Does the school have a (good) formal curriculum?	4	2	0
★*8. Would I have any input in choosing my child's teacher each year?	12	6	0
★ 9. Does the school do well on standardized achievement tests?	12	6	0

_____

★ For the Short Form
* If using this item in rating a school for a School of the Year award, item 8 is "Do parents have input in choosing their childrens' teachers?"

From your look at the school and its classrooms

		Yes	Partially or Not Sure	No
★	1. Are the students spending most of their time on worthwhile activities?	12	6	0
★	2. Are most students working hard yet contentedly?	12	6	0
★	3. Do teachers spend a lot of time interactively teaching groups of one-third of the class or larger?	8	4	0
	4. Do teachers address individual student needs?	4	2	0
★	5. Are many aides and parents working in the classrooms?	8	4	0
	6. Do the teachers seem to care about their students?	8	4	0
	7. Do teachers praise appropriately?	8	4	0
	8. Are the teachers well educated in the subject they teach and in general?	8	4	0
★	9. Are students orderly during recess and in the halls?	8	4	0
	10. Is the principal a good leader of the school?	8	4	0
	11. Is the physical plant adequate?	4	2	0
	12. Do the school's books and equipment seem adequate?	4	2	0
	13. Is the school the regular assigned public school?	12	6	0

From your look at the school and its classrooms

	Yes	Partially or Not Sure	No
14. Is the school convenient to before and after-school activities?	4	2	0

15. Is there any other factor(s) I want to consider in reviewing this school? (Add or subtract points as appropriate)

Factor: _____ ____ ____ ____

If you're scoring and would like to figure out a School Report Card grade for this school, simply add up the points and compare it with one of the following charts:

Standard Form

Elementary School		Junior or Senior High School	
Standard Form: Total Score	School Report Card Grade	Standard Form: Total Score	School Report Card Grade
150+	A	120+	A
130-149	B	105-119	B
110-129	C	90-104	C
90-109	D	75-89	D
less than 90	F	less than 75	F

Short Form

Elementary School		Junior or Senior High School	
Short Form: Total Score	School Report Card Grade	Short Form: Total Score	School Report Card Grade
85+	A	70+	A
75-84	B	60-69	B
65-74	C	50-59	C
55-64	D	40-49	D
less than 55	F	less than 40	F

The School Report Card: Shopping List

Ask
(At a junior or senior h.s., ask the principal or counselor questions 2, 8 and 9 only.)
- ★ 1. number of teachers per grade level
- ★ 2. ability-grouped classes
- ★ 3. classroom aides and parents
-    4. specialist teachers
-    5. schoolwide award system
-    6. schoolwide homework policy
-    7. good formal curriculum
- ★ 8. parent input in choosing teacher
- * 9. achievement-test scores

Visit
- ★ 1. students usually engaged in worthwhile activities
- ★ 2. students working hard yet contentedly
- ★ 3. large group teacher-directed instruction
-    4. teachers address individual needs
- ★ 5. classroom aides and parents
-    6. teachers care about students
-    7. teachers praise appropriately
-    8. educated teachers
- ★ 9. orderly students at recess & in halls
- 10. good principal
- 11. school's physical plant
- 12. books and equipment
- 13. any other factors

★ For the Short Form

CHAPTER TEN

Getting Your Child into the Public School of Your Choice

Give the right reason and persevere a bit and you can probably get your child into any public school in the district.

SUPERINTENDENT OF A PUBLIC SCHOOL DISTRICT

You are not stuck! If your assigned public school doesn't measure up, you may well have a choice other than relocating or sending your child to a private school. From coast to coast, in every district we surveyed, some parents were able to get their child into a different public school, while many others said that they couldn't. In this chapter, we'll share what we've learned from successful and unsuccessful parents, from principals, school district administrators, and from our personal experience, both as educators and parents, to help you get your child into the public school of your choice.

Some parents feel that choosing a public school is somehow wrong. It's not, because it benefits their children. Parents choosing helps better match child needs with a school's strengths, a far better method than being assigned to a school based on one's address. Choice also increases parental support of the school because they choose it.

Parent choice will also benefit society. If parents start becoming active, knowledgeable consumers of education rather than passive recipients, schools will be forced to improve or close

170

because of lack of demand. In other words, market forces would encourage quality in public education, just as they do in the private sector.

Some parents use illegal maneuvers to get their kids into a desired public school—and today, they take a big risk. In the old days, if you were discovered (doubtful), they merely shipped your child back to the correct school with a nasty note attached to his file.

Now they're playing hardball. The front page headline of a recent *Wall Street Journal* announced, "Schools Crack Down on Illegal Enrollments by Non-Resident Pupils. Better Suburban Districts Use Investigators to Sniff Out Any Thefts of Education. The Arrest of Saundra Foster."

Ronald Vitale, an investigator for the Beverly Hills School District, handles about 150 cases a year, using photographs and stakeouts to check residency claims. Recently, he hid a camera in a carton to shoot pictures of a Bel Air family whose children were enrolled in Beverly Hills. What happens when you get caught? Increasingly, you run the risk of ending up like Saundra Foster, arrested, and facing a fine and a jail term.

In addition to legal disincentives, there are important moral ones. For instance, at various times during each school year, a student or his parent must complete forms asking for a home address. If his parent has told him to use a phony address or he see that they've used one, even the most imperceptive child will realize his parents are doing something wrong. This isn't the sort of moral example you want to set for your child. On the other hand, if the child or his parent fills in the correct address, he will probably be discovered and shipped back to his school of residence. He will feel he has done something wrong or that those he trusted have somehow dealt unjustly with him.

Fortunately there are legitimate ways to get your child into the public school of your choice.

What Does the Law Say?

Years ago, unless you went to a private school, you went to your regularly assigned public school. But in the '60s and '70s, parents got more involved in the public schools, discovered that all schools are not created equal, and began to look for ways to get their children into the best ones.

They found that the laws in many states specifically permit children to attend public schools other than the assigned one. For example, the California Education Code, sections 46600 and 46609, states in part:

> The governing board of any school district may admit to the schools or classes maintained in the district any pupil who lives in another school district (when it) agrees it is in the best educational and health interests of the child.

The New York State Education Law, section 2045, states:

> Districts shall not refuse to receive non-resident academic pupils for instruction without valid and sufficient reasons therefor.

In some states, including California, the law specifically allows parents to send their children to school in the district in which they work.

The late 1980s saw further extension of parent choice. For example, all Minnesota children can, subject to some restrictions, attend any school in the state. Many states, including California, New York, Louisiana, Massachusetts, Wisconsin, and Tennessee, have similar programs in place or under consideration. The trend is likely to continue because choice programs have been strongly supported by the Bush administration. President Bush described parent choice as "perhaps the single most promising" school reform idea.

Though not required to do so by statute, many, but not all, public school jurisdictions have formally or informally adopted similar policies, especially regarding school transfers *within* a school district. Districts in states allowing some choice often waive restrictions.

District administrators are ever more fearful of parents filing educational malpractice suits, and of adverse publicity surrounding their less popular schools. Such adverse publicity can result in many parents moving their children from those schools and into private schools. Thus, no matter what policy says, districts often find it expedient to quietly grant individual parents an intradistrict transfer. It costs them nothing to do so.

Even if a school district frequently grants transfers, a district official may try to deter you from applying for one. This is understandable. Admitting that transfers are frequently granted is like admitting that a parent can get a voucher—a practice which could result in overcrowding some schools while others sit empty. If transfers are contrary to district policy, the official will be doubly motivated to deter you from applying.

While it cannot be guaranteed that you will be able to get a transfer in your particular situation, it may well be worth pursuing. For years, parents-in-the-know in many communities throughout the country have been handpicking their children's public schools, a practice that appears to be on the upswing.

Getting Your Child In: Basics

There's no problem getting your child into a school if you've chosen the regularly assigned school. Just go down to the school and register with the secretary. If you and your child's other parent live in different attendance areas, your child can probably attend school in either area as long as he spends part of the school week with each of you.

It can sometimes be easy to get your child into an open-enrollment school, one open to all district children; just be sure to sign up before any deadline. But sometimes there is great demand for an open-enrollment school, forcing the school to turn down some requests. If your request is denied, you're in the same boat as a parent trying to enroll his child in a public school other than the assigned one. Read on.

If you've decided on a school other than the assigned one, but within your school district, you'll need a permit, often called an inTRAdistrict transfer. If you've chosen a school outside the local school district, you'll need an inTERdistrict transfer. The latter is more difficult to get because you need the approval of both the district governing the desired school and your own district, which loses revenue if the transfer is granted.

How to Get an Intradistrict or Interdistrict Transfer

When to Ask

It's usually easiest if you make your request between May and the opening of school in September. That's when enrollments are being planned for the next year, but the numbers aren't yet cast in stone. Unless it's an emergency, don't request that your child be moved in the middle of a school year. It's hard on the child and difficult for the school district, making it less likely your request will be granted.

Whom to Ask

Obtaining an intradistrict or interdistrict transfer is often just a matter of asking the right person and giving a good reason for needing it. Every school district works a little differently, but the right person to ask for an intradistrict transfer is usually either the principal of the desired school or the principal of the school your child is currently attending.

By asking a principal first, you may avoid a district-level procedure, since some districts allow principals to send pupils to other district schools as they see fit. The principal may simply be able to call the principal from the other school and arrange for your child to be admitted.

It's worth seeing a principal first, even if, in your district, she doesn't have the authority to grant a transfer. She may give you advice on how to make your request. For example, in some districts, reasons that "work" can vary from year to year. A principal might know this year's winner. Also, if she sees the merit of your request, you might ask her to put a word in with the person in authority.

If, however, you are requesting an inTERdistrict transfer, it's probably not worth seeing a principal first. Go directly to the district-level person in charge of interdistrict transfers. His office is usually at district headquarters or at least you can locate him from there.

How to Ask

The key to receiving a transfer is the reason you give for wanting it. Give the right reason and the schoolhouse gate often miraculously swings open. Give the wrong reason, and no matter how many school district officials you appeal to, you'll probably get nowhere. Even a sticky lock may open with the right key, but never with the wrong one.

You may actually have many reasons for requesting a transfer: perhaps a series of items from the School Report Card, plus other personal considerations. But giving so many reasons may confuse the issue and vex the district official by giving the impression that you are trying to snowball him with every conceivable excuse. So select one reason that is likely to work.

Acceptable reasons for transfers vary in different school districts. So, before selecting a reason, make a phone call to the district office in charge of granting transfers, ask for the list of acceptable reasons.

However, sometimes districts won't divulge this information. They'll simply say that transfer requests are reviewed on a case-by-case basis. Other districts will provide a list of potentially acceptable reasons, but won't guarantee that they will be accepted.

Therefore, you may find the following information helpful. It is a list of reasons used to obtain a transfer that have proven successful, as reported by parents, principals, and school district personnel in charge of transfers.

Reasons to Obtain a Transfer

1. **Childcare reasons:** if your child, especially at the elementary school level, receives before- or after-school childcare near the desired school. The consensus among those surveyed is that a request based on childcare needs is generally the one most likely to get an elementary school parent's request granted, especially if the parent is still at work when the school day ends.

2. **Program reasons:** if your child needs an important program that is offered at the desired school but not at the assigned school, for example, special education; a particular foreign language; gifted program; advanced placement courses; orchestra or drama if your child is unusually talented; a reading program particularly well suited to your child's needs;

even a sport if, for example, your child is a star swimmer, and only the desired school has a swim team.

A supporting letter from a school psychologist or other educational expert can help get your request granted.

3. **Academic mismatch:** if your child's academic functioning is significantly higher or lower than most of the students at the assigned school. Again, get a letter of support from an educational expert. Note, however, that requests based on academic mismatch are sometimes denied on grounds that children need to learn to work with students of differing ability. Other times, a district will insist that the regular assigned school can and will meet your child's needs and, if you're not satisfied, you must work with that school until you are.

4. **Social adaptation reasons:** your child has had severe problems with students at the assigned school. For example, your child may be picked on incessantly by a group of students; he may have gained a bad reputation (deserved or not) that he can't live down; he may have had an especially traumatic incident at the school (for example, being accosted in the bathroom) which may continue to have repercussions. Once again, try to get a letter of support from a psychologist, psychiatrist, or even a pediatrician.

The following request based on a social adaptation reason was, in fact, granted but will often be denied.

A child was continually ridiculed by his peers for working hard in school. His parent successfully argued, "My husband and I have worked hard to instill in our child a love of learning and a willingness to work. But we know the power of a peer group. Would you want your academically oriented child in a school in which the student norm is to ridicule academic effort and achievement, especially if you saw it already taking a toll?"

5. **Health-related reasons.** Of course, children with physical handicaps are routinely granted transfers to more accessible schools. But there are other less obvious health-related reasons to request a transfer. For example, an asthmatic child

was granted a transfer because the parent explained that the assigned school's poor ventilation was bad for her child's asthma. Another parent was granted a transfer because her child was allergic to the pollen of a particular tree that was widely planted around the assigned school.

Few people who are not similarly troubled realize how sensitive a severely allergic person may be to what seems to be a trifling problem: dust that comes from poor ventilation systems, certain grasses, trees, even smog. These can make the highly allergic child physically sick. You may have to educate the district official about these matters and should get a verifying note from a physician.

6. **Transportation availability and convenience.** One child, who would have had to walk eight blocks through an unsafe neighborhood, often in inclement weather, to reach the assigned school, received a transfer because she could take a bus practically from her front door to the desired school. Another child was granted a transfer to a junior high school twenty blocks from his home when the assigned school was only seven blocks away because her parent explained that her child would have to cross a high-speed thoroughfare to reach the assigned school.

This list of frequently acceptable reasons is not exhaustive. In your situation, another reason may be more compelling.

If you're basing your request on most reasons other than childcare, the importance of getting a supporting letter from an expert, especially one with a Ph.D., Ed.D., or M.D., cannot be overemphasized. Most districts will grant a transfer based on an expert's recommendation, either because they're concerned about the interests of your child, or because they want to avoid a lawsuit claiming your child was harmed when the district refused to follow an expert's recommendation. However, don't threaten legal action. School districts are aware that few parents are willing to spend the time and money needed to assert a possible legal right, fighting a school district's battery of lawyers experienced in just such disputes. Districts may well interpret your threats as empty, the net result being that you lose credibility and make the school less likely to cooperate with you.

Making the Transfer Request:

By now, you've chosen your reason, and you're ready to request your transfer. Don't ask another transfer-seeking parent to accompany you. The principals surveyed agreed that you're more likely to get your request granted if you go by yourself. However, it won't hurt and might help if your spouse accompanied you.

It may be reassuring that you can often get your transfer after one brief meeting, especially if your reasons are childcare or health. Here's an example:

Principal: Please come in. What's on your mind?

Parent: I have a problem I hope you can help me with. I work from nine to five each day. So after school, my son goes to a babysitter who lives just a few blocks from your school. It's practically impossible to get him to the babysitter from the assigned school he's now attending. So I'm hoping I can get a transfer so he can attend this school.

Principal: Unfortunately, we're a bit crowded. Have you tried locating a babysitter near your assigned school?

Parent: Well, no. You see, there's more to it. For one thing, my present babysitter lives right on the way to and from work. That makes it convenient to leave him there on school holidays, but more importantly, the other school is way across town in the other direction from where I work. Also, my son and his babysitter have, for a long time, gotten along well—she is like a grandmother to him. And I'm embarrassed to mention it, but I can afford her—most babysitters charge an arm and a leg.

Principal: I understand. I'll see what I can do. I'll call the principal at your assigned school and let you know either way in a few days.

Sometimes, your meeting with the principal won't be enough to get a transfer, but can be an important step. Often, tact is the key:

Parent: I have a problem with my son [note, she makes it clear she isn't blaming the school] that I hope you can help me with. Gary attended Jackson School last year and, frankly, it's a school year I'd rather forget. Gary came to school a pretty conscientious kid. But his classmates made it difficult for him to keep it up. For example, when he gave a good answer in class, his classmates would mockingly "oooooh," as though giving a good answer made him a goody-goody. On the school bus, kids would make fun of him because he was the only one who took schoolbooks home. Once, they grabbed his books and played catch with them. His binder crashed to the ground and the papers flew all over the street. After a while, he stopped bringing books home and raising his hand in class. His peers started accepting him, but he started to have problems with his schoolwork and attitude. [She has described the problem as objectively as she could, and has been as uncritical of the school as possible, never blaming the teacher or principal.]

I'm afraid that if Gary continues at Jackson School, he'll develop really severe problems. So after considerable thought, I decided to visit your school to see if the same problems existed here at Lincoln. And, of course, they don't. That's why I'm here.

I realize you can't grant every parent's request, but the problem is serious and appears to be getting worse (she has given the principal a valid and compelling reason to grant her request). So, I'd greatly appreciate it if Gary could attend here. I really can't afford a private school, but I'm afraid I'll have no other choice if he has to attend Jackson. [Many principals do want to keep kids, particularly academically oriented kids, in the public school.]

Principal: I'm sympathetic to your problem, but in this school district, you have to apply for a transfer through Mrs. Moll at the district office.

Parent: Do you think it might help if you gave her a call?

Principal: It might. I'll do that.

Parent: Thanks. I really appreciate it. I'll go down to see Mrs. Moll right now. Thank you so much for your help.

What if Your Request Is Denied?

If you choose your reason well and use some tact, you may well get your request granted without major difficulty. But it may be denied for a variety of reasons. Perhaps you chose an overcrowded school, the transfer would further racial imbalance in the district's schools, the district has an unusually restrictive transfer policy, or the officials involved have become so marinated in bureaucracy that they adhere rigidly to "the book," forgetting that "a foolish consistency is the hobgoblin of little minds."

But don't give up! More than one high-level district administrator has admitted that a parent with a good reason for his request and who continues to appeal a denied request, will almost always get it granted in the end. It's usually not worth the district's making a fuss over something as easy to do as putting a child in one school rather than another.

Before going any further, however, carefully consider the reason the district gave for denying your request. Perhaps it is in the best interests of your child to attend the assigned school. But if not, your next step is an appeal. When you receive a denial, the district will probably advise you of your right to appeal and how to make it. If not, simply ask what options you have.

Be sure your appeal includes any supporting letters from experts, and keep a copy of all appeal materials. You may want to hand-deliver your appeal to the person in charge, since your chances are usually better when you deal face-to-face.

Few parents actually appeal, so your chances of getting yours approved are good. But if the appeal is denied, your next and final step still offers real hope. Present your case to a potentially sympathetic school board member or to the superintendent or assistant superintendent of the district. People at these levels have the power to grant your request and often will.

You needn't state your case any differently to these higher-ups, yet your request is likely to be granted. Because so few parents take this final step, top officials have little worry of alienating administrators of the transfer policy or of overcrowding a school.

We know of a high-achieving child whose assigned school was typical of most schools in the district: low-achieving. The parent applied for a transfer to the district's only high-achieving school, arguing that her bright child was unlikely to get an appropriately leveled education at the assigned school because the level of instruction, even in its highest level classes, was far lower than her child needed.

But the district had just adopted a policy prohibiting transfers to the high-achieving school because it was severely overcrowded.

Her transfer request was, in fact, denied. Her appeal was also denied with a letter saying, "This decision is final." But she presented her case to the assistant district superintendent much the way she had in her original transfer request, and he immediately overruled the "final" decision and issued the transfer.

The case illustrates how your child may get into the school of your choice, even when the cards are stacked against you, as long as you are willing to invest some time and if you refuse to be intimidated by the system.

CHAPTER ELEVEN

Improving Your Child's School

Parental involvement is as essential to the ultimate success of the school reform movement as a well-tended mainspring is to the right functioning of a Swiss pocket watch.

BILL HONIG
CALIFORNIA STATE SUPERINTENDENT OF PUBLIC INSTRUCTION

Imagine you could transform the school you've selected for your child into an even better one, not only for your child, but for all the school's children. This hope has inspired many parents to work to improve their child's school. Unfortunately, too often they have experienced more frustration than success. This chapter summarizes the experiences of successful parents so that your efforts can be more rewarding.

What to Improve?

A key to your success is choosing the right goal, a goal that, if achieved, could quickly and enduringly improve the education offered at the school, yet a goal that you, as a parent, are capable of achieving. Focus on one goal at a time. If you're not sure what issue to focus on, you might look at recommendations made in the most recent accreditation or evaluation of the school, and/or do a review of the school yourself using the School Report Card. You may also want to look at the following list of potentially worthy goals to work toward.

Some parents are afraid of being active in the school—needlessly. Children of parents who are active in the school rarely suffer reprisals from teachers. On the contrary, these children are usually treated with special care. And if parents work as a group, the chances of reprisals against a child are even smaller. Nonetheless, because some parents are concerned that their activities may cause reprisals, we have divided the list of school improvement goals into low-risk and higher-risk goals.

Low-risk Goals

- Develop a list of parent resources within the school: parents who are willing to volunteer on a regular or occasional basis in the classroom, talk to a class about their job or avocation, offer a mini- or full course, correct papers, donate items to classrooms, play the piano, sew costumes, chauffeur on field trips, type, etc.

- Develop a list of community resources: the former resident who made it and is willing to tell his story at school; the local bakery offering work experience to the school's students; the computer store willing to train teachers to use a microcomputer; the president of a corporation explaining life in big business; the graduate of a drug rehabilitation program telling how drugs were ruining his life; the city government offering after-school apprenticeships, etc.

- Develop or expand a volunteer classroom aide program using PTA members, senior citizens, retired teachers, members of service organizations such as Kiwanis and the Rotary, disabled persons, high school and college students (who earn course credit). A tough screening of aide candidates, including a trial week of work, is crucial—a bad aide is worse than no aide at all.

- Establish and supervise after-school clubs staffed by parent or teacher volunteers.

- Establish and supervise a telephone "homework helpline" staffed by honor students or parents.

- Establish and/or coordinate an after-school peer tutoring program. (Perhaps with rewards for those tutors whose tutees make progress.)

- Establish and coordinate an annual career day at the school in which employers set up booths, and classes come to see presentations and ask questions.

- Sponsor parent workshops on parenting, improving children's reading, math, study habits, etc.

- Raise funds for purchases that wouldn't otherwise be made by the school or district. One use of such funds is paying for teacher-of-the-year awards. You can use the Teacher Report Card on page 133 to determine the winners. (Such awards tend to have the greatest positive effect when twenty-five to fifty percent of teachers receive an award each year.)

- Provide large numbers of student awards for best and most-improved achievement, service, and citizenship.

- Sell copies of parent/school materials. An excellent selection is distributed by the following nonprofit organization:

The National Committee for Citizens in Education
10840 Little Patuxent Pkwy.
Columbia, MD 21044-3199
Phone: 800-NETWORK

In addition to providing useful resources to parents, such sales can generate profits that can be used to benefit the school.

Higher-risk Goals

(These should be undertaken by an organized group of parents.)

- Get a parent on the committee that hires a principal or teacher. Schools sometimes take a passive approach to recruiting and screening teachers—they simply interview the few people sent down from the district office and choose one. Given that union contracts virtually guarantee the new teacher a job for life, the parent member(s) of the committee should ensure that recruitment and selection be more thorough—for example, aggressively seeking outstanding teachers from other schools, and calling universities to get the names of highly recommended graduates, then observing final candidates actually teaching if at all possible.

- Ask the principal to agree to a formal policy that allows parents input on selecting their children's teachers.

- Encourage the principal to make teacher evaluation and improvement a high priority. While getting the principal to take these actions requires considerable tact, it is one of the most important goals a parent group can achieve. The existence of just one incompetent teacher at a school means that for many years to come, thirty children each year are likely to suffer boredom, chaos, lack of learning, and damage to their attitudes toward school and self. Yet because of the time and stress involved, principals rarely make efforts to fire such teachers. Thus, parent influence is essential.

- At the high school level, encourage the school to send all parents a letter inviting them to review their child's academic and career direction with the school counselor. Too many students take courses that end up not being in their best interests. When they're seniors, they discover that they haven't taken the right courses for college admission, or that they stayed in the pre-college track even though they would have been better off in a vocational one.

If you've decided to make your school-improvement efforts as part of a parent group, first find out if an appropriate group already exists. The Parent-Teacher Association is a logical first place to look. Many PTA's focus their efforts on important school-improvement issues. But if your PTA doesn't, perhaps there is a more appropriate smaller organization at your school.

If no such group exists, you can limit yourself to individual effort, or be willing to make the significant but potentially rewarding effort to start your own "Parents for a Better School" group. A wonderful pamphlet, *Parents Organizing to Improve Schools*, provides in plain English a practical guide for starting such a group, and is available from the National Committee for Citizens in Education.

Almost always, the most effective way to bring about change is through the combined efforts of parents and educators in a true spirit of cooperation. In the '60s and '70s, militant parents tried to challenge the school establishment and take major control of schools. These efforts rarely helped children, and it is now widely agreed that such confrontational approaches don't work. Both educators and parents must work together to effect change.

This doesn't mean that parent groups should always function as school officials would like them to. Sometimes educators relegate parents and parent groups to peripheral roles like organizing teacher appreciation luncheons, decorating the gym for the dance, and raising funds that educators alone decide how to spend.

The appropriate balance is usually found when parents share with the principal and other school personnel their ideas about needed improvements at the school, and then engage in a respectful dialogue about the validity of those goals and the means to achieve them. To ensure success, make sure that a concrete plan with a timetable is agreed to in writing, and that follow-up is planned.

Only as a last resort should you go over the principal's head. Some savvy parent groups wield considerable latent power by reporting *positive* things to district officials, school board members, legislators and the press. Most principals will realize that if positive things are reported, the negative ones could be, too.

When their all-too-short years of childhood are over, you will recall with no small satisfaction that you made the effort to get your children a good education. These efforts, which later will seem so small, may emerge as among your most rewarding.

INDEX

NOTE: In an effort to ease locating references of interest, subentries have been listed in order of appearance within the book.